THE RAINBOW TABLETS™
DIVINE UNION AND SACRED SEXUALITY

Channellings from the Rainbow Race

SIA-LANU ESTRELLA

ISBN (paperback): 9781662926938
eISBN: 9781662926945

Library of Congress Control Number: 2022939268

The Rainbow Tablets™
Divine union and sacred sexuality
Published by Gatekeeper Press
www.GatekeeperPress.com

Contents

Dedication

This book took me on a life journey more poignant and powerful than I could have ever imagined. I offer my deepest gratitude to my amazing dad. Without you, I never would have made it through. You were my rock, my guide and my best friend. Now you continue to be so from above. Thank you for supporting me in bringing this sacred remembering back to Earth.

To all of the amazing friends and soul family who helped me through this period of my life, I am so grateful. Your prayers and healings for my dad were so powerful and appreciated. I thank you from the bottom of my heart for the compassion, friendship, hugs and laughter.

Thank you to Lesley Myburgh for helping me to unlock my gifts and become the person I am today. I especially appreciate everything you gifted me in those last months I lived in Peru.

Thank you to Auqui Jaquehua and Juvenal Crispin. You taught me so much about the depth of sacred ceremony and working with the wisdom of the land. Our times on the mountain are forever in my heart.

Thank you to Ben Borg for being the most amazing brother. I look forward to even more adventures and service with you throughout the world. I love you so much, so much.

Thank you to Donna Byatt for receiving me in England with open arms, and to you, Steve and Milo for being my family abroad. Your friendship has been such a blessing in my life.

Thank you to Carol Haddad for being such an incredible space holder for this work. I am eternally grateful that our paths crossed and for the adventures we have shared, as well as those still to come.

Finally, thank you to each and every amazing soul who reads the Rainbow Tablets books and works with me through the deeper activation and embodiment offerings. This cosmic wisdom is incredible and empowering beyond anything I've known. But it cannot change the world alone. This remembering must be embodied. Each of us who chooses to heal ourselves and come back to divine love and wholeness within, creates the change. We anchor the Rainbow Frequency – our All-essence. And we ripple it out.

Without you, these books would just be words on a page. But through your embodiment, you are literally changing the world and co-creating the Great Awakening. I honour you.

Preface

Welcome to the second of The Rainbow Tablets books. Each manuscript is a transmission of powerful cosmic remembering. Now that we are in the Return to Unification, this cosmic wisdom can finally be restored to Earth. We are calling it back to ourselves. As each of us comes back to wholeness within – our Rainbow Frequency of divine love – we create the new Rainbow Earth. We are literally changing the world through our own embodiment.

As a channel, I write in such divine flow that I do not fully take in the wisdom until I read it myself. This book has touched my soul in a profound way. From my teens, I knew there was something very 'off' about the way we experience sex and relationships on Earth. My heart told me it was so much more sacred and magical than what I saw everywhere I looked. I longed to experience a union that felt in resonance with that truth. But I was unable to find a man who could meet me there. What's more, I had much to heal and awaken within myself before I could truly access the remembering of divine union and sacred sexuality.

I am now so excited to share this manuscript with you. For so many, it will feel like the missing piece – the knowing that you always felt but could not quite access. For others, it may be challenging. But I trust that all who are led to this manuscript are ready to free themselves from the old distortions and unlock the magic and sacredness within themselves and their relationships.

Read this slowly or devour it. Whatever feels right for you. I invite you to come back to it many times. Each time you will understand it at a deeper level. The transmissions from the Rainbow Race are always encoded to assist you in coming back to your true essence. But the transmission will only share at the level that is right for you at any given time. When you come back to the manuscript at different times, you will access more of the codes and activate more within yourself.

If at the end of this manuscript, you feel the call to awaken and embody your Rainbow Frequency – your All-essence, please gift this to yourself. I spent most of my life keeping myself small. When I finally committed to walking my highest path and answering the call, immeasurable magic, blessings and joy flowed into my life. When we say 'yes' to living our highest expression, the universe supports us in ways that exceed our wildest dreams. Just in case you need to hear this – you are worthy.

The Rainbow Race have had me channel amazing offerings to support you in unlocking your greatest gifts and returning to wholeness within. You can find these on my website at: www.sialanuestrella.com

And please tell everyone about this book. Do not keep this to yourself. The yearning for 'something more', something 'forgotten', resides deep in the hearts of many. If you receive something from this manuscript, tell everyone you know about it so they can also receive these gifts. Imagine how quickly the world can change when we consciously ripple out the remembering.

Everything in this manuscript is channelled from the Rainbow Race, our Rainbow Unified Selves, except my personal stories. As it was with the first book, I was guided to share with you my own journey as I embodied this remembering and birthed this book. My stories appear in the introduction, the start of each section and the epilogue. Some names and details have been changed to protect privacy.

All that you read in this manuscript is brought through in greatest purity. Before I channel, I come into ceremony and open sacred space. I have trained and worked in these ways for many years. As you may know, I lived in Cusco, Peru for three years. For me the sacred is not just something to do every now and then. It is how I approach every day and everything I create. I genuinely believe in living life as sacred.

Now, I invite you to open your heart. I wish you an expansive and transformational journey with this remembering!

A message to me from the Rainbow Race about the reason these manuscripts were brought into being:

"It is time to open the gates. These are the gates to wholeness, unification, divine love. This is the Rainbow Frequency – the biggest uniting force in the multiverse. Now is the Great Awakening; the Great Remembering. The Return to Unification. It is the way to end all suffering, all separation, all duality and all 'time'. This is the period of remembering your divinity.

"The Rainbow Tablets teachings had been bound for eons. But now we are in the Return to Unification. All old contracts can be annulled. The time of duality and separation is over. Hundreds will awaken by the day. You can now bring yourselves into unity within.

"The Rainbow Tablets teachings are not and can never become a doctrine. They are a deep remembering; a cleansing of all old forms of control and manipulation. They are the restoration of purity, empowerment and wholeness. They are the remembering of your essence of divine love."

Introduction

The sweat dripped off the end of my nose as I strained to inhale against the searing heat. My lungs burned and I dipped my head slightly, determined not to lie down. Not yet at least. It was only the third 'door' of the traditional Mexican sweat lodge, the Temazcal. We still had one more round after this one, and each was always hotter than the last.

The drum reverberated off the low and curved ceiling. It made my chest shake. Images flashed before my closed eyes. Ruins and jungle. The high-pitched call of the Temazcalero medicine man reached into the ethers, summoning the ancestors. Suddenly they were flooding in. Ixchel was the first to greet me. She stood on a Maya temple. Not surprising given I was here on her land. Next the lion's face and my Lyran star family came in strongly. I smiled and the rocks hissed as the Temazcalero threw more water on them. A wave of intensified heat hit my body and I rocked back and forth as I tried to breathe through it.

Out of nowhere, Wiracocha appeared and I gasped. While living in Peru I had seen his image in Inca temples and on touristy gifts. Never before had he appeared to me. His face was powerful and close to mine. He said nothing, but I knew he was bringing my Peruvian connection and that of the great Apus, the mountain spirits.

The Temazcalero's voice rose. In the pitch black, I heard someone on the other side of the stone pit start to sob. More hissing and more steam. It was almost too much. When would this door end? My ears strained, waiting for the sweet release of the word, "Puerta!" But there was only more drumming. And more hissing.

I called my focus back to myself. Back to my intention and purpose. I had come here to heal. To release the almost crushing grief of losing my father. He had been my rock. My best friend. My safety net. He was the one who had truly loved me unconditionally. Now that he had moved on from this plane, I did not want to be here. Everything was different. The world felt hostile and jarring. I was so alone.

A few years earlier, I had been at a star gate in Peru with my twin flame. The red rock formation was so out of place in the flat green and yellow planes. It was like an alien landscape. I had repaired codes in the portal and reactivated the star gate. It brought such a sense of familiarity. I knew I had passed through that portal countless times.

My star family had thanked me and offered an invitation. "You have already done so much. If you want to come home, you can pass through the star gate." They gave me the instructions. The gate was not where people thought. But I had looked down the hill and seen my twin flame sitting on the ground with his shoulders hunched. He had looked so lost. In so much pain. Whatever challenges lay ahead, I knew I could not leave him.

Now it was three years later and things were different. The intensity of the heat and drumming pushed me deeper within myself. It had taken 10 months to heal the scars after I ended it with my twin flame. Then a roller coaster of cosmic weaving had unfolded to relocate me during a 'pandemic' with closed borders. Then my father had gone for a routine colonoscopy and they perforated his bowel. He had fought so hard for close to a year. Over 20 surgeries. Until his heart valve gave out. He had made it through that surgery. But his lungs had never recovered from being on the respirator for so long.

We had let him know that it was ok to let go if it was all too much. But he had wanted to fight. And we had supported him every step of the way.

In those last weeks when my dad had one foot either side, he pulled back the veil and helped me access higher-frequency planes. The gifts had flowed into my work. And just a few hours after I channelled the last transmission of my Rainbow Starseed Activation Program, I got a video call. It was time. At exactly 3.33am by English time, my mum dropped Dad's hand and called his name. She stood and placed her fingers on the pulse point in his throat. Then she clasped her hand over her mouth and wailed.

The intensity of the memory jarred me into the present moment. The heat was stifling. Sweat dripped down my neck and chest like a torrent of tears. My whole body was crying as the grief released. He was gone. My guide and best friend was gone. And I knew where there was a star gate in Peru. I could leave Earth if I wanted to.

Did I want to? I was only two-thirds through channelling the second Rainbow Tablets book. I knew this remembering was needed on Earth. But was that enough of a reason to stay?

Suddenly, the falcon-headed Egyptian being, Ra-Horakhty, appeared before me. The golden sun disc that glowed behind his head was almost blinding. And although his piercing eyes could see right into me, they were filled with softness. Like a father's love.

"Your father stayed much longer than he was meant to," Ra-Horakhty said. "Do you remember when he almost died when you were eight years old? Then again in your 20s? And again in your 30s?"

I did remember. Vividly.

"These were all moments when he was meant to cross over. But he didn't. He stayed for you. This time he could not put off his work any longer."

The song of the Temazcalero sounded like a Shamanic wail. I wanted to wail with him. My heart ached and vibrated as the medicine drum shook up all the things I had not wanted to acknowledge.

I wiped my face and neck with my sarong and exhaled deeply as I closed my eyes once more. Ra-Horakhty was waiting for me.

"Your Earth father was your guide and guardian. But he was not your purpose. That is yours and yours alone. You know what it is. It is bigger than you and your dad. Now it is time for your galactic fathers to step in and guide you."

The air was damp and fiery. I gulped it in as Ra-Horakhty presented me with a crown of blue jewels. I knew I had worn it before. And he told me he was also my father.

I thought of that moment back in Peru when the Rainbow Race had revealed my destiny. They had shared that I was the Rainbow Tablets and had held these codes for eons. It was all waiting for this moment. The time when it was right to restore the remembering. The Return to Unification.

I gently bounced my crossed legs in the unbearable heat. And I remembered my promise. I had told them I would see it through – whatever was asked of me. I had given myself in highest service. The hiss of more water on the stones sent out a scorching blast of steam. I brought my hands to the ground and ducked my head so my ears would not blister. Still I faced the question. What would it be?

I was two-thirds through the second book, 'The Rainbow Tablets: Divine union and sacred sexuality'. Already I had been shown the third, fourth and fifth books. Could I really give up and bail out? What about my promise to the Rainbow Race? To Pachamama? To Great Spirit? To myself?

A Lyran lion appeared right before my face and roared. Instinctively, my heart and soul roared with it. There it was! My inner fire – the Lyran courage.

"I'll stay," I whispered. I felt the ancestors and my star families rejoice. Their belief and support brought new tears – tears of relief.

In that moment, the Temazcalero ceased drumming. Then he yelled, "Puerta!"

Section 1

THE RETURN OF SACRED SEXUALITY

The sky had an eerie red glow and ash rained down. My heartbeat quickened. Were we supposed to evacuate? Should I grab my parents' dog and go?

I glanced along the cul-de-sac. The neighbours' cars were still in their driveways. Surely my dad would have called if the alert for their area had been upgraded. Trust me to come home to Australia in the midst of the worst bushfires in years. Calling to the dog, I went back inside and looked out the back window. A family of kangaroos was feeding nearby. The alpha male stood tall and scratched his belly. It was funny the simple things you missed when you lived overseas.

A familiar beep interrupted me and I grabbed my phone. Maybe it was my parents with an update. It wasn't. I hit play on the voice note from a friend in the United States.

"Hey, so I just need to let you know that Ro'Kay paid me a visit. He's just floating around up there and says one of you needs to embody him. Apparently he needs to be embodied on Earth before the end of the year. Just lettin' you know. Ok, love ya!"

For the second time my heart started to race. But this wasn't about the bushfire. It was the big elephant in the room that I had been ignoring. Or perhaps I should say, the Lyran lion in the room.

During my first trip to my twin flame's country, we had both felt a strong connection to our Lyran higher selves. What we had been waiting for our entire lives had finally emerged. One windy night, we had taken cacao to the beach to sit in ceremony. As I channelled, I was given the names of our Lyran higher selves – Hakhmet and Ro'Kay.

Yet, when my counterpart chose not to walk his path, it had thrown us both into new timelines. I had embodied Hakhmet. She was a Lyran Queen and Goddess. But her King had been left on the higher planes, because my King had not stepped up.

A few months before I flew to Australia for Christmas, Ro'Kay had appeared to me. He wanted me to embody him. I told him I couldn't. It felt like a betrayal – like I would be taking something from my counterpart.

3

"Don't you see," he had said gently. "We are all one. All four of us are fragments of the same Rainbow Unified Self. Yes, it was the intention that you would embody Hakhmet and he would embody me. But only one of you has answered the call. It is always the risk when one comes to Earth that they will become lost in the distortions. Yet the work must continue. I cannot tell you what is coming, but I am needed on Earth. You must embody both of us and hold us in divine union within you."

It had all been too much. My loyalty was too strong. Yet, when I heard the voice note from my friend, I felt the sense of urgency. It was less than a week until the new year. The Rainbow Race had insisted the first Rainbow Tablets book be available from the start of the new year. It was right on track.

I poured a glass of water and watched the kangaroos hop into the bush. Somehow I felt the truth of it all. Ro'Kay did need to be embodied. And it did need to happen now.

I picked up my phone and unblocked my counterpart's number. My friend was also a friend of his. So, I told him of her message and asked if he was willing to embody Ro'Kay. Surprisingly, my phone beeped just a few minutes later. I had my answer.

"Alright," I said, feeling into Ro'Kay's energy above. "Let's do it."

Five days later, I was lying on the floor of my dear friend's healing space. It was the thirtieth of December. And it was our third breathwork session. The first two had released so much resistance and grief. This whole situation had forced me into the final acceptance that I was doing this mission alone. My counterpart would not be taking part. Well, at least not in his human embodiment. But the wisdom he was meant to carry still had to be brought through. I was holding the Lyran Queen in her beautiful divine feminine essence. She needed to be in union with her King. That had led me to this moment.

The smell of ceremonial tobacco filled my nostrils as a cloud of mapacho enveloped my crown. I opened my eyes to see my dear friend, Dan, leaning over me. He blew a single puff over each chakra. Then he placed his hand on my arm.

"Are you ready?" he asked in his gentle voice.

"No."

Dan laughed as he stubbed out the mapacho in his abalone shell. "Come on. I've been in the desert in Mexico with you. I've seen what you can do. You've got this."

I smiled. If anyone knew how to hold me through huge multidimensional work, it was Dan.

"Ok," I said and exhaled loudly.

Dan guided me into the breathwork. As always, he gave me plenty of space to lead my own journey. He supported with the medicine drum. His voice was ancient and wise as he sang. Tears streamed down my face as I felt Ro'Kay hover above me. Yet, as he tried to merge with me, I was still resisting. I could feel the need to open my heart and energy field to welcome this loving higher aspect of myself.

I groaned and my body convulsed. "I need more mapacho," I said.

Dan put down his drum and blew mapacho over my energy centres. Then he moved to my palms and the soles of my feet. I could feel myself opening. But I was still fighting within myself. What if this meant that was it for my counterpart and me? What if I was losing him forever by embodying what we were meant to hold together?

Dan shook the rattle over me and the limitations started to break apart. It felt like I was being torn and I screamed. This was not about my counterpart. He had already made his choice. This was about me – my expectations and attachment to how it was 'meant to be'.

I groaned and jolted as I consciously let go. Dan moved effortlessly from mapacho to drum to rattle, whistling and singing as I fought within myself. Was I going to truly walk my highest path? Or was I going to hold onto what would never be?

"Keep breathing. In … and out. No break. You've got this."

Again, I screamed. I hit the ground with my fist. But something opened within me. It was like a rush of ecstasy as I broke through the barrier. And I finally let go.

As Ro'Kay entered my being, it was like golden honey. Warm and smooth. My heart opened and the feeling of bliss amplified. I saw him in all his glory. His beautiful strong lion face. His glowing crown. And I saw Hakhmet alongside him. She was white and had her rainbow wings outstretched. A sense of peace and wholeness washed over me. I was only vaguely aware of Dan's gentle whistling in the background as he rattled to help seal my energy field.

The power within me was both transcendental and fully-grounded. The two Lyran aspects of myself came into divine union within. And I felt whole in a way I never had before.

* * *

*"At the highest levels of sacred sexuality, you can live and create as 'orgasm',
as the 'God' that you are and as one with all around you. Rather than
'having' an orgasm, you become an orgasm — the breath and being of all creation
itself. This is the meaning of divine union, within and with another.
It is to live in wholeness as the divine, as the All-essence."*

Sacred sexuality

In the higher levels of sacred sexuality, you create as nature itself. You call in the earth, air, fire, water and rainbow. You become completely one with your physical environment. And you create as the elements themselves. All responds to your will, and your will is love. For only those operating through the purest Rainbow Frequency can access these highest levels of sacred sexuality.

Here 'sex' is creator force. There is no need for touch, either self-pleasure or with another. However, you can choose to do so for sheer pleasure, delight and co-creation.

Through the highest levels of sacred sexuality, you become creation itself by merging with the elements. Only when you have come back to purity, moved beyond ego, will the elements merge with you. They will be drawn by your purity. It is different to 'controlling' the elements. Through this merging with the elements, they become you and you become them. There is no hierarchy of power, but rather you create together as one.

When you do this, you allow the creator force 'sexual energy' to move through you. To create through you. You become a channel and beacon for the creator force energy. You become 'God' - The All. It is the memory of your essence in its purest form, and the reconnection with this essence in all around you. It removes all separation. In this state there is only oneness. All is one.

At the highest levels of sacred sexuality, you have already embodied divine union within. You have remembered your wholeness. So, sharing your life with another is a choice, not something you feel you 'need'. It is a choice to amplify this wholeness by co-creating with another 'God' force alongside you.

When you become divine love once more, which is what you always were, you stop 'needing' love. Relationships are no longer about fulfilment, but rather a celebration and co-creation. It becomes more about what you can give to each other and facilitate the co-creation of, rather than what you want or need from each other.

Through the re-embodiment of the highest levels of sacred sexuality, an orgasm is not a 'moment' or climax. It is a state. A frequency. It is a way of being. For an orgasm was never a human physical experience. It was a moment of tapping into the divine – like touching 'God'. Not God as something external, but God as within you; God as connection with all things. An orgasm was a moment of oneness.

At the highest levels of sacred sexuality, you can embody this state. You can live and create as 'orgasm', as the 'God' that you are and as one with all around you. Rather than 'having' an orgasm, you become an orgasm – the breath and being of all creation itself.

In this way, when you come into practice with another, it becomes like two universes making love. It is all creation experiencing itself through another. The love and power are boundless.

This is the meaning of divine union, within and with another. It is to live in wholeness as the divine, as the All-essence.

So, how do you obtain these highest levels of sacred sexuality? Through embodiment. It is through re-embodying your Rainbow Frequency and rising above egoic love into cosmic love that you can once more experience yourself as all of the cosmos. We share about re-embodying the Rainbow Frequency in 'The Rainbow Tablets: Journey back to wholeness'. And we have passed embodiment programs through the Channel to assist you with this.

In this manuscript, we take you deeper into this embodiment in relation to your sacred relationship with your gender, sexuality, divine union within and divine union with another. You are soon to see that much has been done to keep you from this greatest embodiment and expression of your divine creator force. But this is the time for you to reclaim and restore it for yourself and all on Earth.

When you create your reality using your creator force, there can be no karma. We will share more about moving beyond karma later. But essentially, at these higher levels, you have remembered yourself as The All – as creation itself. And when you create from the Rainbow Frequency, it can only be love.

Through this creation, there is nothing you lack. All flows effortlessly, because you are creating as the creator force; as creation itself. That is why it is the highest and most pure form of magic. You literally become the divine love essence, all of creation. Whatever you choose to experience really is a choice. You are the creator. You are co-creating all in your reality.

When you experience yourself as The All, you also experience all others in this way. You see and experience The All in everything. It is the purest way of being. And when you see and feel from this plane, you realise there is nothing onto which you must hold. In every single moment, only one thing is true – the All-essence of divine love. It is the only constant. No matter what race, dimension or star system. Therefore, divine love is the one truth. It is the essence that makes up you and every single thing in existence, including time and space itself.

The highest level of sacred sexuality is also the key to moving through time and space. Because, when you become the Rainbow Frequency of divine love, you realise that you *are* time and space. You are The All and all is one.

It is also how you cure all sickness. When you remember that The All is everything, you remember that everything is love. Every single cell. Disease stems from disconnection and separation. It is the belief that one cell is different to another and that one cell can attack another. But when you remember that all is love and love is all, dis-ease ceases to exist. All separation within is restored to wholeness and divine love, the All-essence. It is the end of all illness.

Embodiment of the Rainbow Frequency of divine love, and divine union within is how you hold paradise within. And when you choose to create using the highest levels of sacred sexuality, it is how you co-create paradise on Earth.

Accessing sacred sexuality

We know that the human pattern is to be given the answers. A series of steps to follow. 'Do these five things and you will achieve the desired outcome.'

The highest levels of sacred sexuality cannot be shared in this way. It can only be accessed through embodiment. This means that it cannot be taught. We know this can feel frustrating for the human mind. But remember that we are not operating at that frequency. The concepts and remembering that we are sharing with you have been kept from humans for thousands of years. This is a much higher frequency than anything you have previously encountered in this lifetime. Therefore, it cannot be reached through the mind. It can only be reached through the heart.

You will remember that in the first manuscript we shared that the heart is the pathway to everything. The heart is the portal. Yet, the heart must be pure. A heart that holds pain, trauma, barriers and separation cannot access the deep remembering of the greatest magic and weaving of your creator force.

It is through your return to wholeness within and your Rainbow Frequency that you will unlock the secrets of sacred sexuality. It is something that can only be remembered through experience. Through embodiment. Through awakening something within that is so pure and cosmic that it cannot be translated to words. You *live* into the remembering.

So, you may wonder what we are sharing in this manuscript if we cannot reveal the intimate details of how to practise the highest levels of sacred sexuality.

The answer is: the key. We are sharing with you the remembering and the key to unlock it for yourself.

As well as the big-picture cosmic remembering, we will gift you grounded tools and practices to bring about embodied change. This will prepare you to step into sacred sexuality and unlock its magic.

We will expose the illusions, showing you the programs, distortions and ploys of control and disempowerment that are at play to keep you away from this remembering. This will empower you to liberate yourself.

We will take you into the deep and powerful remembering of divine union. This will show you how to embody divine union within and with another.

We will restore the remembering of the divine purpose and role of gender and sexuality. And we will unveil the greater mysteries around the womb and pregnancy as divine co-creation with the cosmic realms.

All of this will reawaken the essence of purity and power that is beckoning you. The greatest and most pure magic. The act of living and creating as creation itself.

A journey into the cosmic mysteries

As we have shared, the highest level of sacred sexuality is beyond simply a moment of touching the divine during a point of climax. It is an embodied experience of becoming 'orgasm'. Of vibrating at the frequency of creation itself, the All-essence. This is the full embodiment of your Rainbow Frequency and weaving it as the great master that you are.

This is what was meant by the Cosmic Rainbow Prophecy when it was foretold that the 'Gods' would walk Earth once more. These 'Gods' were never going to be external beings. Rather, it was each of you claiming and re-embodying your All-essence.

That prophesised time is now. The remembering is ready to be restored.

Perhaps you can already feel that what we are sharing with you through this manuscript is a transmission. It is woven with the codes to help you remember. To help you to unplug from the sex distortions and parasitical programs. To help you reclaim the power of divine union and sacred sexuality in its highest, most cosmic form.

We begin the manuscript in this way, so you understand what it is that you are about to receive. This is the key. This is the unlocking of all that is your birthright as a great cosmic being. When we say 'birthright', we do not just mean in the human form you currently assume. Rather, we mean that this is your right from the moment your essence was birthed as an 'individual' fragment of your Rainbow Unified Self.

This is what the whole experiment in separation – a period of eons – was leading to. It was all about this moment of realising that you were never separate. This moment of realising that you are the All-essence. And the remembering of how to create as creation itself.

This is the 'holy grail' in a sense. What all have been seeking. This was the root of that stirring inside you that you felt since childhood. The sense that you had forgotten something. The sense that there was something so much 'bigger' and more magical.

It is why you have felt that there was more to sex. Why you have yearned for something 'more', even if you could not express what that was. It is why you may have felt that, no matter how great your sexual interactions were, there was something missing. Never reaching a sense of complete fulfilment or satisfaction. And it is why, so often, sexual chemistry fades over time.

We know that this pathway back to your pure essence and the sacred can be a little daunting. As we have shared before, it is a process of shedding all that you are not in order to re-embody all that you truly are.

Just because we cannot share a step-by-step manual, we do not wish for you to worry. You will be fully held on this journey back to wholeness and the remembering of divine union and sacred sexuality. The pathway to this remembering is through your Rainbow Frequency. We have already shared courses and activations through the Channel. And we are continuing to share through her, creating a full embodiment journey for you. So, your remembering and re-embodiment is fully supported.

With this in mind, we invite you to relax. Exhale any worries that you are not worthy or ready. You are. Ask your ego and rational mind to step aside. Some of the things we will share may be confronting because the old disempowering programs are so woven into your society. But we ask you to read on from the heart. For, if you allow yourself to feel and 'experience' the remembering, it will awaken the great purity within you.

Now we invite you to journey with us into the great mysteries of divine union and sacred sexuality. With this key, you can unlock the greatest cosmic truth and power that you hold within.

Section 2

THE NEW RAINBOW EARTH

The sound of hammering ricocheted off my walls. I shut off the video and stormed upstairs. I had lost count of how many videos had been ruined from the renovations. We had a schedule. I had offered to do all of my work on three days a week, leaving the landlord four days to follow his whim of building another apartment above mine. Yet, for over five weeks now – ever since the lockdown had started, this had been a daily battle.

"Manuel," I called out. He put down the hammer and looked at me with his usual smirk. There were two sides of Peru. There were those who would give you the shirt off their backs, even if it were the only shirt they had. Then there were those who looked for every opportunity to screw someone over, especially foreigners. Especially female foreigners. 'Gringas'. This is where I found myself.

"Por favor, sabes que hoy dia es el dia que necessito trabajar," I said, raising my palms in exasperation.

His smirk spread to his eyes. With a dismissive shake of his hand, he said he was going to build whenever he felt like it. If I didn't like it, I could find somewhere else. He knew, of course, that it was not permitted to move house during this extended military lockdown. I went back to my apartment, shaking from the injustice of it. Two years I had lived here. When I moved in, Manuel had told me this was a quiet place and a 'family' home. It was exactly what I was looking for. But I had soon discovered that it was all on his terms.

How was I meant to share multidimensional journeys and mentorships with electric saws and hammering in the background?

I stood looking out my window. The snow-capped peak of Ausangate glistened in the sun. He was the most sacred mountain in Cusco and my most powerful guide. "What am I meant to do?" I asked him.

"It is time to move."

I rubbed my face and sighed. Great. Even my most trusted guide and guardian had lost the plot. It was almost impossible to find long-term rentals in my area. With Airbnb, landlords could make more from tourists staying thirty per cent of the time than having a reliable long-term tenant. Ausangate knew this. Plus, there was the whole insane lockdown situation.

My bed creaked as I flopped onto it. The banging overhead continued and I reached for my Florida Water. I couldn't let Manuel get to me. I was the creator of my reality. That's what three years of living in Peru uncovering the cosmic wisdom had taught me. It was time to take control.

I lit my sage and the billowing smoke instantly shifted my frequency. Gathering my sacred objects, I prepared for ceremony. Usually I would have done this outside. But in five weeks I had only managed to get my bare feet on the grass once. It had lasted a whole three minutes before a police officer was standing over me.

I placed my potted Wachuma cactus in the centre of my desk. If I couldn't get onto the land, I would connect with Pachamama through Grandfather Wachuma.

After strengthening my Rainbow Pyramid sacred design, I dropped fully into my heart. I was at a crossroads. This hadn't been my original timeline. If my counterpart had stepped up, I would have moved to his country months ago. Without marriage, there was no way to get my residency there. I knew my time in Peru had come to an end, but the next phase hadn't dropped in yet. It was like being in limbo.

The Cusco basin looked so still. The streets were empty. The usual sounds of firecrackers, car horns and parades had long been silenced. It felt like the whole country was in limbo with me.

"I call in my highest timeline," I said out loud, connecting with my intention as I offered ceremonial cacao and mapacho to the Great Mother and Great Father. I buried them in the soil of the pot and felt warmth in my heart.

Through my third eye, I saw my highest timeline trying to drop in. It hovered over the Andean mountain range before me, like a tornado that had not quite touched down. How strange. Why wasn't it landing?

I closed my eyes and turned my attention within. Why was my highest path not supported? Instantly, I felt the response. "It is."

I placed one palm on my heart and the other on my womb. What was it then? What was blocking me from moving forward? Through the stillness, I drilled deeper until I found it. The outcome. I had released the desire to be with my counterpart. But I was still longing to move to his country. The dolphins and manatees often came to me in dreams. And the waters seemed to be woven into my soul.

The first time I had stood in the townhouse my counterpart rented on the bay, I had recognised it. I knew we had planned this home and section of the bay to start our lives together. It wasn't him I was holding onto. It was the waters and the animal messengers.

With deep love and respect, I told them I could not come and needed to step into a different timeline. It was hard. They kept calling me. But I promised to visit when I could. Then I removed all chords and contracts.

When I opened my eyes, my new timeline touched down. I seeded my intention without expectation. I was ready to leave my beloved Peru.

As I anchored this new possibility, something else rose to the forefront. It was time. The second book was ready to come through. 'The Rainbow Tablets: Divine union and sacred sexuality.' I had been told this before. But I hadn't officially accepted the calling. Was I really capable of bringing through an entire book on that topic?

Even as I questioned it, the knowing rested deep inside me. This was something I had longed for since I was in my teens. This remembering needed to be restored to Earth. If the Rainbow Race was calling me to channel it, I had to say yes.

A little jar of red liquid caught my eye. It was an offering I had gathered in my moon cup yesterday. Years ago, a sister had first told me about moon time ceremonies. I had been repulsed and rejected it instantly. Then she said something that had made the hairs on my arms stand on end.

"The Indigenous grandmothers are asking all women to remember. We used to bleed onto the earth. It was a way of giving our life force back to the Great Mother. And it kept everything in balance. Then society taught us to be ashamed of our moon time. They developed products to dispose of this life force," she had said.

"The grandmothers believe that this created a grave imbalance. They say that when enough women return to gifting the blood of life to the Great Mother each month, the blood of man will no longer need to be spilt."

It sounded crazy from a Western point of view. But from an energetic perspective, it felt right. As uncomfortable as it had been at the time, I had switched to a moon cup. And the monthly ceremonies had brought me into deeper connection with Pachamama, myself and the divine feminine.

I picked up the small container. If I was going to commit to a whole book on such a powerful topic, I was going to need to put my life force behind it. I accepted the call and grounded my intention. After the ceremony, I sat back in shock. Something huge had shifted. Closing my eyes, I saw that the new timeline had now touched down. I could feel it. It was more grand than I could have imagined. And it felt so tangible.

"Look now for your new home. It is on Airbnb. And do not worry about the lockdown. I will shield you." Ausangate's wisdom filled my heart.

With disbelief, I browsed the app. It had never occurred to me that all the tourists had left at the start of the lockdown. Within minutes I found the perfect place. I contacted the owner and arranged to see it that afternoon. I already knew it was my new home. And it would be the start of a whole new Rainbow timeline.

* * *

*"When you create using the creator force sexual energy,
you are creating as love itself. And everything you bring into being is of love.
Therefore, through this embodiment, you transcend karma."*

The highest expression of Earth

At the start of the experiment in separation, before all across the cosmos collectively agreed to enter the Reign of Darkness, Earth was a paradise for the Gods. It was a place they came to forget, just so they could experience the delight and bliss of remembering once more that they were The All; that they were divine love. And they came to create.

Yet, once we entered the Reign of Darkness and all remembering that we were The All was removed, Earth changed. It became a competing ground for energetic control. Parasitical beings tampered with the human DNA and implanted disempowering programs. Societal structures and Governments were founded on this.

This you know from 'The Rainbow Tablets: Journey back to wholeness.' But we recap to set the scene.

Now that we are in the Return to Unification, Earth is being restored to paradise once more. It begins through your embodiment of paradise within. And divine union within is key to returning to paradise within.

Let us take a moment now to share with you what this Rainbow way of life on Earth is like. It may seem like an impossible utopia. The truth is that this utopia already exists. As you know, all time is happening at once, for lack of a better way to describe it. The Earth that existed before the Reign of Darkness (and still does exist in that point in time and space), is this utopia. The future Rainbow Earth that you are working towards, also already exists. So, what we share today is not a fantasy, but a reality in other points in time and space. And you are being invited, through your own embodiment, to bring it into being in your reality.

With that said, we now invite you to imagine an Earth founded on love and unity. It is a place where all are aware that they are sovereign beings, and they recognise the sovereignty of all others. Each has brought the divine feminine and divine masculine into unity within. They do not experience a battle within between their 'light' and 'shadow'. Rather, they have recognised that these were but two halves of the divine love frequency of unity. So, they have embraced all that they are and have become whole within themselves.

These humans are also aware that they are of the stars, as are all others. They are multidimensional beings who have had (or rather, 'are having') lifetimes in many dimensions and timelines. They are aware that they have chosen one of those experiences to be on Earth in human form, and they see it as a beautiful gift. They are the embodiment of divine love; the expression of the All-essence, as is every other being. And they are able to connect and work with the other fragments of themselves in other dimensions and timelines (sometimes referred to as 'higher selves'), with great ease and grace.

Because these Rainbow humans recognise the divine in every other being, they do not project expectations or blame onto any other. They see the connections they have chosen – mother, father, brother, sister, friend, colleague and so on – as a gift. It is an opportunity to co-create with other beings to form the highest expression of their service. It is not about obligation or old definitions of the roles of certain relationships. Rather, it is a beautiful landscape for co-creation. The purpose and intention of each being is to serve, express and co-create. There is no greed or deception. For there is no competition. The purpose is not personal gain. Through the exploration and co-creation of all that their heart desires to experience in this great paradise, each feels deeply fulfilled.

When two come together in union, it is divine union. They come together as two whole beings and expressions of the divine love Rainbow Frequency. Their purpose in union is to lift and inspire each other, and to experience the All-essence in each other. There are no struggles for power. For each knows that they are whole within. So, there is nothing they need to draw from the other, for there is nothing they lack. And there is no temptation or infidelity.

For, in divine union, two souls are attracted to each other for their highest co-creation. Each knows that any romantic or sexual interaction outside of the union would only lower their frequency. And because their core purpose is to bring into being their highest service, this would be against their desire and intention.

When two in divine union choose to bring through a Rainbow Child, they recognise this as a sovereign being with its own innate wisdom. They do not feel the need to dominate, control or indoctrinate the child. Rather, their purpose as parents is to provide the most loving and nurturing environment for this sovereign being to grow into their highest service. They welcome and nurture any new gifts or remembering that the child brings from the higher realms.

In this time of utopia on Earth, there is no separation. Therefore, there is no religion. These old frameworks disintegrated as more and more awoke to the remembering that they were 'God', the All-essence. As was every other being. In the same way, there is no tension, exclusion or judgement between races. Rather, each is embraced as a dear brother and sister. Skin colour is obsolete. For, through the embodiment of the Rainbow Diamond Frequency and the interweaving of the Golden Abundance Codes, the humans of Rainbow Earth have skin that is luminescent and shimmering with these frequencies.

Animals are no longer slaughtered or abused. They are recognised and celebrated as dear guides who play an important role in the co-creation of paradise built on love, magic and unity.

In this Earth as paradise, wealth and abundance are not stockpiled by a few. When there is no greed and no competition, there is no need to have more than others or hoard more than one needs. Those who do choose to acquire more than they need act as redistributors, helping those with less. The Lyran Golden Abundance Codes (the Arraya pure abundance consciousness) have been restored to Earth and woven through the fabric of the new societal structures. There is no fear of lack because it is known that the multiverse is all-abundant. The good fortune of one does not mean that another must miss out. Yet, some may choose that they wish to experience and create from more humble means. While others may desire a more luxurious experience on Earth. Each is a master creator, so they can weave the experience they desire.

Methods of exchange have evolved. At times it may be expressed in a form of money. Other times it may be through time, wisdom, skills or magic itself. And exchanges do not always have to be direct. This is a concept some refer to as 'paying it forward'. If one has enough, they may offer their services and ask the recipient to gift the energy exchange to another. Those who take on the role as redistributors open to receive larger amounts of abundance, so they can share it and amplify the weaving and work of others. This is not the same as charity. For the recipients are not in a place of need or desperation. Rather, it is an expression of co-creation where the highest service of one as a redistributor of abundance, ripples out to support the highest service of others.

Again, this is all part of the embodiment of co-creation and unity. There is no separation. Every single being is an expression and embodiment of The All. Therefore, all are family. All look out for each other. Kindness, compassion, generosity and unconditional love are foundations of paradise on Earth. All is in flow. And all are connected to the ever-flowing infinite abundance of the Arraya pure abundance consciousness. This is the fabric of co-creation that makes up the multiverse. Kind and generous acts always flow back – not because that was the intention, but because acts and gifts of love and abundance attract more of the same.

All have remembered that the greatest purpose is co-creation. Through their unique highest service, they are able to add to this highest co-creation. Each person's gifts are honoured and valued. Difference, or for a better description, uniqueness, is celebrated. It is understood that each person brings unique gifts. And each set of gifts is needed for the collective highest good – the highest co-creation. Old ways of trying to make one conform are long gone.

The Great Mother is honoured. Without greed and disconnection, the ways of over-producing and over-consuming are from an old time. Instead, each is conscious of what they need and consume. All associations of status being linked to having the 'latest this' and 'latest that' have dissolved. For they were based on ego and lack of self-worth. One only needed validation or status through their possessions when they felt inferior or unworthy within. As each came back to the embodiment of divine union within and their Rainbow Frequency, they realised there was nothing they lacked. They saw that every other being – human, animal, plant and so on – was their equal.

As each came into this remembering, they felt the Great Mother as the wonderful being and consciousness that she was. Once this connection was re-embodied, it became impossible to abuse or pillage her. Each became more conscious and responsible about what they used and purchased. Because all in existence comes from the Great Mother. It is taken from her flesh and her children. Just as you are her child, so is every animal and tree and droplet of water. This deep reconnection with the Great Mother as a loving being, made each realise that everything they used or took from her, affected her. If one is truly in their Rainbow Frequency of divine love, they only use and take what they require. And it is done with deep love and gratitude, often giving something back in return. All is in balance and harmony.

What is more, each is having an experience as the All-essence. They are aware that they are the expression of The All, and everything they create is of the essence of divine love.

When one feels they have expressed all they wish for that incarnation, they may choose to leave. In this actualisation of Earth as paradise, 'death' is simply the sovereign being's decision to move onto the next experience. In this way, there is no need for traumatic deaths, natural disasters, murder or disease. These were all symptoms and effects of being in separation; of living in unawareness that each was The All. That said, one can still choose a different experience of departure if they wish. This would only be where they felt the experience was an important part of their learning and highest expression. Therefore, this is quite rare.

As we have said, this is not a description of a fantasy world. It is the Rainbow Earth that already exists in what you would perceive as the past and the future. Now you have the opportunity to bring it into being. Yet, as we have said, paradise without starts with paradise within. And the pathway to paradise within is through embodying divine union.

Transcending karma

To create using the highest levels of sacred sexuality, one must first re-embody their Rainbow Frequency of divine love. When they do, they transcend karma. This may seem impossible, but allow us to explain.

Karma was an energetic form that was there to serve your highest good. It was never about punishment, as some believed. Rather, it was there to guide you back to your Rainbow Frequency – your divine love essence. Anytime that one acted in a way that was less than love, karmic laws came into play. Essentially, a lesson would be shared with the being to assist them with growth and remembering, so they could find their way back to embodying divine love.

Due to the density of energy, time and space during the Reign of Darkness, many of these karmic lessons were delayed. Often, they would be delivered in the next lifetime. We know this may seem confusing because we have shared that all time is more or less happening at once. But this is not strictly the case, for it would imply a never-ending time loop. The language does not exist on your planet to describe these more intricate layers of multidimensionality. So, we do the best we can with the language available.

The only way to end the experiment known as the Reign of Darkness was for enough beings across the cosmos to remember that they were in fact The All. They were divine love. As more and more came into this remembering over time, it reduced the density of the energy across time and space. In this way, karma gradually became less of an experience for the next lifetime and more often something to be experienced in that same lifetime.

As even more across the cosmos re-embodied the All-essence, time and space became increasingly less dense. It reduced the distinction (blocks) between timelines and other dimensions. This made it possible for beings to heal and clear karma not only in their own timelines, but across other timelines.

Some of you on Earth have been working in this way. As we shared in the last book, part of coming back into wholeness is collapsing other timelines and calling other fragments of your Rainbow Unified Self back together. This does not mean you cease to exist here or in another timeline. Instead, all fragments of yourself feel a greater sense of wholeness and embody more gifts and remembering from their other timelines.

You may recall that we shared the image of a paper chain of people to represent fragments of the one Rainbow Unified Self. You are one of these fragments. As you collapse timelines, you embody gifts and wisdom from other fragments, leaving each of you feeling more whole.

When the paper chain is folded (representing the return to your Rainbow Unified Self), it becomes a single sheet of paper once more. But the individual cut out people do not cease to exist. We understand this may be a little difficult to grasp, but we ask you to surrender to the knowing that there are many concepts or complexities of multidimensionality that we cannot explain in the Earth languages.

We also know that it may seem strange that we switch between present and past tense. This is because we, the Rainbow Race, exist in wholeness outside of time and space. To us, where you are in time and space is 'the past', even though you experience it as 'the present'. Do not concern yourself with these little things. Multidimensionality is something to feel and remember rather than something to understand.

So, let us take it as a given that you are able to clear karma not only within your current timeline, but across other timelines. As you return to wholeness within, you remember that you are The All. You are the divine love essence. When you re-embody this, you transcend karma. For, as we have shared, karma was only there to help guide you back to your divine love essence. Once you have re-embodied your Rainbow Frequency of divine love, everything you say, do and create is from this essence of divine love. And when you are acting from divine love, there is no more karma.

You may wonder what this has to do with the highest levels of sacred sexuality. Well, one can only use the pure magic of the creator force once they have re-embodied their Rainbow Frequency of divine love. At the highest levels, it is not about 'sex' as you know it. Rather, it is about how you channel the creator force energy to create and manifest as the 'God' that you are. Every single star, being, animal, plant and so on in existence is the All-essence. There is no separation between you and The All, or The All and anything else in existence.

When you create using the creator force sexual energy, you are creating as love itself. Everything you bring into being is of love. Therefore, through this embodiment, you transcend karma.

The new role of twin flames

We have already shared much about this topic in 'The Rainbow Tablets: Journey back to wholeness'. Now we wish to delve deeper. Some of what we are about to share may seem quite new and different to what you have heard in the past. This is because when we entered the Return to Unification, everything changed. It brought (and continues to bring) accelerated shedding, growth, embodiment and remembering for many.

To recap, twin flames are two fragments of the same Rainbow Unified Self who chose to incarnate into the same timeline in order to speed up their return to wholeness. These pairings have a pre-designed greatest mission. When they come together, even if just briefly, they activate codes within each other. This connection can take the form of parent and child, siblings, friends, business collaborators, romantic partners and more. As it is most common for this dynamic to play out through a romantic union, and divine union is the focus of this manuscript, this is where we will place our focus.

Although the highest expression of the twin flame connection is often divine union with each other, it is not imperative for the attainment of their highest paths. When two incarnate into separate families and lives, they have their own experiences. When they are brought together, they may or may not be ready for each other, and ready to unlock their deepest remembering. In many cases, one or both may still have some things they need to heal within themselves.

The frequency of twin flames – being two fragments of the one Rainbow Unified Self – is one of absolute purity. When they come together, the frequency of one will push to the surface in the other anything that is not in alignment with truth and purity. And vice versa. This can be a very intense process and it requires great presence, compassion, surrender, trust and co-creation. If one resists or is not willing to meet oneself (both in their current incarnation and in the incarnation as their twin flame), it can cause great tension and disharmony. In some cases, it can become destructive, especially to the one who is willing to step forth into their highest service.

It takes a conscious decision to show up and 'do the work' if the twin flames are to make it through this process and come into lasting and loving divine union. This is absolutely possible. There are those enjoying the power and beauty of coming into loving union. It can feel like a love and magic beyond anything they imagined. And often there is a sense of knowing this is an outcome they have been working towards for many lifetimes.

There are also those who have tried and parted ways, but will reunite in the future.

Then there are the unions where one twin flame is not willing to liberate themselves from the distortions. In this case, staying can become destructive

27

for the partner. Often, the only way for the partner to reach their highest service is to leave the union. This can be a difficult experience, for the vows between twin flames run deep. And they exist through multiple timelines.

But, as we entered the Return to Unification, there was a great cosmic shift. As we have shared, it became possible to transcend the old framework of karma. It also became possible to transcend old contracts and create from the new.

As we collectively stepped into the Return to Unification, it propelled all across the cosmos onto new planes. It opened ways of experiencing and creating that had been closed for eons. And it empowered you to rise above the old ways of being.

A twin flame pairing in your current timeline, also exists in many other timelines. Although a twin flame pairing may not be able to move into successful union in this timeline, in all likelihood, they are in successful union in another timeline. Often this is in what you would refer to as a 'higher' dimension. In truth, there is no hierarchy between dimensions or fragments of yourself. But we are limited to the language with which you are familiar.

Once the great shift happened, a decision was made about twin flames on Earth. This decision was made by the very same twin flames in successful union on the 'higher' planes. So, it was made by 'you' (in a 'higher' timeline) for 'you' (in your current timeline).

This decision was that where it was no longer for the highest good of the twin flame pairings on Earth, the vows between them could be removed. In these cases, another divine union partner could be called in if it was desired. So, there has been a great reshuffling of pairings. It is a huge reconfiguration of highest timelines.

In order for these new highest timelines to anchor, each must clear and release all expectation and attachment to their old timelines. Where they hold on, they keep themselves in a lower timeline and tied to karma. Each chooses their own path. Now that we are in the Return to Unification, the presence and playing out of multiple realities is more evident than ever before. One who is or was anchored to a 'lower' or 'older' reality with their twin flame, cannot bring in a new greater divine union until they release the old and choose their new highest timeline.

Holding divine union – within and with another – is one of the highest forms of service on Earth. It is how you restore Earth to paradise. To support this, timelines are more fluid than ever. They are constantly realigning to serve your highest good. In the collapse of so many intended twin flame unions, incredible cosmic weavings are taking place. New connections are being brought into being that combine codes from different star systems. It is an opportunity to bring together great wisdom, gifts, remembering and magic in new combinations.

For those who have had to release vows with their twin flame, this is not failure. The ultimate purpose of twin flames is to activate codes within each other and fulfil the highest mission. If you are following your highest service, you have not failed – not on any level. Nor has your twin flame, even if they have chosen a lower path. Free will and the veil of amnesia on Earth meant it was always the case that some unions would not come into being. And when you release all blame, expectation and attachment, you allow yourself to return to cosmic love. For this is the true essence of twin flames. It was never one of obligation, but rather a cosmic love that is far beyond any frequency of egoic love.

When one releases their vows with their twin flame because union is not for their highest good, they surrender to the divine. They can call in their new highest divine union and receive a partnership beyond anything they have known or experienced. Entering such a union with one who is not your twin flame in no way reduces the expression of divine love and co-creation between you. In fact, what you can create with your new divine union will surpass anything that would have unfolded from remaining in an unrealised or destructive twin flame union.

In this way, regarding twin flames and divine union, the highest vow you have taken is always to yourself. For you and only you can choose to be in your highest service. You can never force another to grow or remember. But your highest service is so greatly needed, that the universe will do everything to support your success. As you re-embody your Rainbow Frequency of divine love, you create as the All-essence. So, you can bring into being whatever you wish. It may not be in the form or with the specific person you had envisioned, but that in no way detracts from its purity, bliss and success.

Section 3

REMEMBERING DIVINE UNION

There wasn't a single cloud in the sky. It was the kind of blue that felt like it went on forever. I raised my hands joyfully as I blew mapacho towards the never-ending space beyond me, honouring my star families and the Rainbow Race. Ausangate was whiter than usual, as though he were beaming his love to all of Cusco. It felt amazing to be in the new apartment. The roof area was a huge blessing after so long in lockdown.

I took another puff of mapacho, continuing my ceremony to open space for my first multidimensional retreat online. They were all with me – Isis, Osiris, Horus, Thoth, Anubis. Sekhmet, the Lyran white lions and the Rainbow Race. And, of course, Ra-Horakhty. We were meant to be in Egypt right now. It was an amazing group from all over the world. We had been looking forward to it for months. With borders closed, it wasn't possible.

"You will bring them anyway," Sekhmet had told me. "We have much to share with them and it cannot wait."

So, here we were. I had managed to negotiate a full refund for the group and offered to deliver the retreat every day as a gift, following our itinerary. It was our third day. Already I was blown away by how powerful this work was. Many rainbows had graced the skies during our live sessions. Not today though. Today the sky was a clear expansive portal to the great mysteries beyond.

"You must be my new neighbour." The voice surprised me. "I'm Raphael. I live in the apartment beneath you."

I smiled and quickly introduced myself. He was tall with a shaved head and skin only a little lighter than his black t-shirt. He rubbed his chin and continued chatting as he stepped towards me. I raised my hand. "I'm so sorry. I'd love to chat later but I'm in ceremony at the moment. I'm just about to run an online retreat."

"Oh, yeah, no. No worries." Raphael nodded and went back downstairs. I felt bad. I didn't want to be rude. But I was starting in ten minutes and had to finish opening the space. Bending down, I stubbed out my mapacho and used some Florida Water to drop back into the space. Later I would say hello properly. But right now, we were about to journey.

Almost two hours later, after closing the sacred space, I stretched out my arms with joy. The session had been incredible as always. We were literally at the temples having real-time multidimensional experiences with our Sirius and Lyran brothers and sisters. Sekhmet told me this was 'just the beginning' of what I would share in this way.

Just then I heard footsteps from the stairwell. It must have been Raphael. I rushed to the door.

"Hey, I'm so sorry about before. I hope that wasn't rude. It's just that I was starting the session really soon."

Raphael nodded and we moved past the awkwardness. He was from London and had come to Peru for four days. That was just over six weeks ago now. Her literally only had four changes of clothing. We laughed at the craziness of it all. Then Raphael commented on the number of rainbows he had seen since I moved in.

I smiled. "Yeah, that's because of the work I'm doing."

"What *are* you doing?" he asked. "I can feel really powerful energies coming down from your apartment. It's awesome – like a free medicine journey!"

I laughed and explained. Then I handed him a copy of my first book to read. He said he couldn't wait to start reading it, then continued down to his apartment.

A few days passed before I bumped into Raphael again on the roof. He gushed about the book and the multidimensional experiences it was triggering for him. I laid in the sun while I listened. It was nice to talk to someone in person. For weeks, my only interactions had been with my wonderful clients over Zoom. Or trying to reason with my old landlord in Spanish. Raphael and I realised how isolated we had been until now.

Weeks passed. We were both busy. Him with projects. Me with my online retreats and the second book, which I had well and truly started channelling. It was fun to take time out to chill on the roof and chat each day. Our conversations were fascinating. We regularly had to announce a 'to be continued' before we ended up spending the entire afternoon together and forgot about work.

"Do you want to hear something crazy?" Raphael asked one day.

"Always!" I said with a grin.

"I've been here before. These mountains. This outlook. It wasn't exactly the same as this, but very similar. It was about a year and a half ago. My guides started coming to get me and would take me along a rainbow highway to a location. One of the guides looked like you, actually. But she was older. Maybe that's why you feel so familiar to me."

"Wow, that's so cool that you ended up here in real life too."

He nodded in amazement, then took a drag of his cigarette as he tapped on the rail of the rooftop area. I was glad I had never smoked. Even when I puffed mapacho, I only drew it into my cheeks. Somewhere in the distance a sheep bleated. And I rolled up my yoga pants to get some sun on my legs.

Life was strange. I had been living here for four weeks now. Just that short time ago, Raphael and I didn't know each other existed. Now, apart from our sweet Peruvian landlady and her brother, we were the only ones we each saw.

"Hey, do you want to hear the latest channellings?" I asked.

"You know I do!" Raphael sat on the ground at a ninety-degree angle from me and impatiently tapped my ankle with his foot.

"I'm going, I'm going," I laughed as I grabbed my laptop and opened the file. "Ok, this section is all about divine union."

"Oooo, yeah! Lay it on me."

Reading the channellings out loud was like hearing them for the first time. When I typed, I only retained about thirty per cent because it was such a pure flow. But when I read it back, I had the full experience. My heart expanded. Goosebumps climbed my legs and arms. It was everything I had felt from my teens but had not been able to articulate. And I could feel there was so much more to come.

I spoke the last line and looked up. Raphael was shaking his head and laughing.

"This. This! That's what I'm talking about. Damn, you better keep writing because the world needs this!"

I smiled. It was so nice to hang out with a man who understood divine union. Not only did he understand it, but he was hungry for it. He had been wanting to experience it his whole life, but never had. I could relate to that.

"Was it like that with your twin flame?" he asked.

"Far from it. Like here to Australia and back fifty times kind of far." I laughed. Yet there was still a pang in my heart. The channellings were not how it had been with my counterpart. But they were how it was meant to be. It just never came into being.

"How about you? With your ex-wife?" I asked, nudging his foot with mine.

He rubbed his chin. "Nah. That whole thing was hostile. On our first date I knew she wasn't right for me. Somehow, eight years later I was walking down the aisle. Everything inside me told me it was a mistake. But it was like the thing had its own momentum."

Raphael paused to finish his cigarette.

"That's why I came to Peru. I needed to find myself. Because somewhere in all of that… I don't know where I was."

I flopped back onto my yoga mat and stretched my arms above my head. The cement was hard under my back. But the sun felt amazing on my skin. The whole world was in turmoil. Yet somehow, I was in a sacred little bubble on the side of an Andean mountain, channelling cosmic wisdom from the Rainbow Race.

The words about divine union were still pulsing in my heart. There was a choice before me. I could feel that Raphael was interested. And maybe I was too. He was great. Really great. But I didn't feel ready. The pain of the experience with my counterpart had cut so deep that I didn't know if I would ever be 'ready' again.

I put my hand over my heart and sighed out. This was one of those moments. Another layer of healing. A time to dig deep. I couldn't let this one experience prevent me from ever experiencing divine union with another. It wasn't about Raphael. It was about me. I had already embodied Hakhmet and Ro'Kay. I was holding them in divine union within myself. But I hadn't truly come into that frequency.

The only way I would know if I wanted to start something with Raphael or not, was if I was whole within myself. The answer and liberation were in my divine union within.

* * *

"True divine union takes commitment. Yes, there is the commitment to the other that you will show up, hold space, honour and love them. But more than that, is the commitment to yourself. This is what so many miss. They make it all about the other person and forget that divine union with another is actually the external representation of their divine union within."

Divine union and the All-essence

As we have shared in 'The Rainbow Tablets: Journey back to wholeness', at your essence you are divine love. You are the Rainbow Frequency. You are whole – the embodiment of The All experiencing itself in this experiment of separation.

Perhaps it is some time since you read the first manuscript. Allow us to briefly recap. In the beginning, there was only The All. Then The All wished to witness itself, so it broke apart into the Rainbow Race. These are beings of light with the Rainbow Frequency of divine love (the All-essence), running through them. They exist outside of time and space and are completely whole – no gender and no birth or death, for there is no time.

After some time, it was decided to have a deeper experience. So, each Rainbow Unified Self broke apart into many fragments, of which you are one. Time, space and dimensions were created to give form to the experiment in separation, for it was never intended to be forever. Much time passed and it was agreed to enter a great experiment known as the Reign of Darkness. Duality was created and the knowing that each was the expression of The All was erased. It was agreed that the Reign of Darkness would only end when enough across the cosmos had remembered that they were The All – the Rainbow Frequency of divine love.

Precautions were taken by encoding chosen Lyran God and Goddess pairs with The Rainbow Tablets. And they agreed to be bound so the remembering would not be returned until the experiment was over.

When the quotient of collective remembering and re-embodiment of the Rainbow Frequency occurred, the Reign of Darkness ended and, across the cosmos, we moved into the Return to Unification. The Rainbow Tablets were unlocked and restored to Earth, for this deep remembering belongs to all. The beacon of the Rainbow Phoenix was activated and made visible in all parts of the multiverse. And inter-galactic relations flourished, bringing the remembering and Rainbow Frequency to star brothers and sisters who had long been in the dark.

This is the time of unification. It is the remembering that all is love and love is all.

Now the truth of divine union and sacred sexuality is being returned to Earth. This is your highest embodiment; your greatest expression of yourself as creation itself. For, as we will share, divine union is not just an externalisation of two coming together. Divine union exists within. To come into your highest magic as a channel of the creator force energy, you must first embody divine union within. It is your purest frequency, your greatest wholeness. It is the act of experiencing yourself in wholeness within the plane of separation. And it is your birthright – the greatest reward for having moved through the experiment of the Reign of Darkness and having emerged whole.

Some say they are the light. But this is not so. This is like saying they are but half. This is the experience of being in separation and duality. Light and dark are but two parts of the whole. When they are brought together, the result is divine love.

It is the same for the divine feminine and the divine masculine. They are two halves of the whole. Yes, you have chosen a physical embodiment and this should be honoured with the deepest gratitude, for it is the sacred vessel you chose from which to experience this remembering. But, within, you are both the divine feminine and the divine masculine. When you unite them through divine union within, you restore yourself to the Rainbow Frequency – the All-essence. And it empowers you to shape your experience through the creator force that flows through you.

As you read this, perhaps you may wonder if being whole within will make you androgynous or sexually ambivalent. This is not the case and there is nothing to fear in truly embodying divine union. You will not lose who you are. Rather, you will be able to re-embody all that you ever were, at your highest and most whole frequency. And you will be able to walk Earth as a God. For that was the original purpose of Earth. It was the playground of the Gods. It was paradise. And you are returning it to that now.

Gods are not hedonistic or vengeful. This was all part of the old distortions and programs inflicted on humans to keep them disempowered and in fear. Rather, Gods are all-loving. They are giving and nurturing. They are connected with all that is. They are the embodiment of divine love and see this in all others. They create their own experience for their highest good and that of all. To live as a God is to live as one with all that is.

This is what you are restoring to Earth. This is the great remembering, the great return to unity. It is unity of all living things on Earth, and the unity of all races – Earth and stars.

And your greatest power starts with divine union.

The history of divine union

Thousands and thousands of years ago, when we agreed to enter the experiment known as the Reign of Darkness, it offered an opportunity we had never known before. As our Rainbow Unified Selves, we were whole. There was no gender and we were the divine love essence in its most complete form. All was love and love was all. So, there was no such thing as 'loving' another or 'being in love'. We were love. Love was everything. There was no other state.

When we experienced duality and separation for the first time, we were able to experience love as though it were outside of ourselves. Of course, the purpose of the experiment was always to return to our divine love essence within. But this would be a journey of eons. None could have anticipated how long it would take. Yet, as we have shared, the purpose of it all was experience. And we have certainly had that. We experienced pain and hurt and hate. We experienced joy and ecstasy and love. Throughout the experiment and the many, many lives we took on, we experienced the fullness of all that was.

During this time, we felt love as something that could be and not be. We thought it was external to ourselves. Therefore, it was something to fall in and out of. We thought it was hard to maintain and cultivate, that it took hard work. We had forgotten that love was, in fact, what we were. We had forgotten that love was not something to feel, something fleeting, but that it simply 'was'. Love was the force that made us exist. Love was the source of every cell. Love was our essence.

As we have shared in the previous manuscript, some star brothers and sisters struggled more with the experience of being in separation. They felt so deeply cut off from the creator force, forgetting that it was within them. They turned to the darker end of the experiment in duality. They fed on pain and the pain of others. And they tampered with Earth and the human DNA.

There are also those star brothers and sisters who chose not to feel at all. They found the experiment and experience too much, so they adjusted their own DNA to remove all feeling centres. They became emotionless, without empathy. They did not feel, so everything became scientific for them. Without feelings to engage with the experience, they turned to simply studying it and their fellow star brothers and sisters, from a scientific view. Over time, this led to experimenting on others.

This is not about appointing blame. All were having their own experience with the sense of separation and duality. And all are in the process of remembering their Rainbow Frequency and coming back to wholeness. So, to avoid naming specific races, we will simply refer to the star races that inflicted the tampering and programs onto Earth and the human race as 'parasitical beings'.

As part of their tampering, these parasitical beings implanted sexual distortion programs onto Earth. They knew that the most effective way to cause pain and suffering in humans was to cut them off from their connection with the higher realms.

Sacred sexuality was one of the most powerful ways for beings to remember their divine love essence. It was a practice that was only performed within sacred divine union. And, at this time back in the early days of the Reign of Darkness, divine union flourished on Earth. It was through this sacred container of love and unity with another, that the love one felt for the other would be reflected back. In that moment, one would see the other as divine love. And, in doing so, they would remember themselves as divine love.

It was also during these early days of the experiment that humans and other loving star races were working together. They were delighting in this rediscovery and remembrance of love. And the ability to experience this love in dedicated union with another was euphoric. It provided the moment of remembering the All-essence within. Through divine union and the act of sacred sexuality, each pair was able to open a portal directly back to their Rainbow Unified Selves and The All. It empowered them to bring the purity of this frequency to their current plane. And it unlocked the pure magic of using one's creator force.

Our fallen star brothers and sisters who were suffering with their experience of being in separation saw the joy and bliss being experienced on Earth. They were filled with resentment and infiltrated Earth. We do not wish to go into all the details, for these atrocities have been forgiven. But they claimed Earth and humans as their own and banished the other loving star races from having contact. This division held for a long, long time.

The parasitical beings shortened the human DNA and implanted the sexual distortion programs. Some incarnated as hybrids and they spread the sexual distortions like a disease. They separated sex from divine love and divine union, bringing it into a purely physical realm. Rather than the pleasure of connection and re-embodiment of the divine, it became about pleasure of the skin – a parasitical feasting on another's energy. They also brought in practices of many people engaging in disconnected sex at once, so none could see the divine reflected in another, for there was no true intimacy and no sacredness.

It went further than this, into very dark places, that formed the basis for some of your Earth problems today around sex trafficking and paedophilia. We do not wish to delve further into this. Suffice to say that the fallen brothers and sisters succeeded. They all but erased the remembering of divine union and the highest levels of sacred sexuality from Earth.

With this connection lost, humans could not find the divine love essence within themselves. They fell further and further into pain and suffering. Wars raged. Greed flourished. The parasitical beings fed on the helplessness and depravity of humans. Earth became a feeding ground for the lower beings. All seemed lost.

However, even as all of this was happening, there were those in higher realms and other star systems who were remembering and re-embodying their divine love essence, their Rainbow Frequency. The shift towards the end of the Reign of Darkness and into the Return to Unification was taking place, even though it had to occur over thousands and thousands of years. Star Councils were formed. Some who were further along in their remembering took on roles as Ascended Masters. They gave themselves in service to help others remember their own divine love essence, and that all was love and love was all.

Back then, the grids around Earth were almost impenetrable. Sending high frequencies from above was not possible. So, some of the great masters from the high councils agreed to incarnate on Earth. Sadly, their lessons were twisted and formed into doctrines that were used to enforce control and separation.

But all was not lost. The secret teachings of divine love and sacred sexuality lived on. It was guarded by star gates and Ancestor Star Keepers who chose to remain on Earth in spirit form. Therefore, the energy was secretly woven into some of Earth's sacred places, ready to be released and activated when the time was right.

Flash forward to your time now and, as you know, much has changed. Millions of great masters have chosen to incarnate on Earth. They dismantled the old lower-frequency grids from the inside. Now Earth is able to receive high-frequency transmissions from the higher-dimensional planes.

Those great masters who incarnated on Earth carry the remembering within them. Although they had to forget when they passed through the veil of amnesia, many are re-awakening by the day. And it is now that the loving star races are sharing the transmissions of divine love and the highest levels of sacred sexuality to Earth once more.

As divine union returns, each will once more be able to see the divine love All-essence in their partner. And, in having that reflected back, they will see this in themselves. It is through divine union and the return of sacred sexuality, that each will remember and experience themselves as the God that they are. This can also be experienced through solo practice for those who do not have a partner. We will share more about this.

It was always prophesised that the Lyrans would walk Earth again and that when they did, they would destroy all illusion. This is why the channel incarnated and agreed to share the Rainbow Tablets. It is time to dismantle the old parasitical sex distortions. No longer will humans be duped and disempowered through addiction to parasitical ways of purely physical pleasure and unsacred sexual depravity. Now humans will be gifted the secrets of the higher realms once more. Through their embodiment of divine union – both within and externally – they will remember that they are Gods. They are divine love. They are the All-essence. And all are one.

Holding divine union within

Many are aware of the concept that in order to love another unconditionally, you must first love yourself. This is true. But we wish to take you beyond this now and talk about divine union within.

Firstly, there are two pathways to divine love with a partner. One is as we have just shared, first loving yourself fully. The other is when two come together and make a commitment to return to divine love together. In your current experience on Earth, this is more common. It is the acknowledgement that each partner is still healing, shedding and re-embodying. They are on their path back to loving themselves, as is their partner. The two choose to take the journey together, honouring themselves and each other as they move through the layers.

This is a beautiful commitment and process and we will talk about this more later. For now, let us say that divine union is far more expansive than many realise. Most have only experienced this with another. But divine union is something that you hold within. It is the perfect union of the divine feminine and divine masculine within. For some, this will be enough. There is no rule to say you must experience divine union with another or that you have somehow failed if you do not. So, we will share about both – divine union within and divine union with another.

Before we go further, we wish to say that we will talk in terms of the divine feminine and the divine masculine. This is energy and consciousness. It is not to be confused with gender. Regardless of the physiological form, each holds the divine feminine and divine masculine within. And when we talk about divine union within, we talk in energetic terms of the feminine and masculine. This may or may not be reflected in the physical forms of each partner. By this we mean that divine union at this time on Earth can be experienced through mixed-sex or same-sex union.

Wishing to find and experience divine love with another is one of the most pure intentions one can hold. It is a sublime experience of witnessing The All in another and having them reflect The All in yourself. Coming together to co-create as two embodiments of the divine love creator force is a truly magical expression.

However, the tampering with human DNA and Earth's grids cut humans off from this expression. For thousands of years an egoic form of love and union has prevailed. It has generally started with glimpses of pure expression, but soon spiralled into control dynamics, blame, expectations, deception and so on. Often neither has felt that they could fully express who they were.

True divine union takes commitment. Yes, there is the commitment to the other that you will show up, hold space, honour and love them. But more than that, is the commitment to yourself. This is what so many miss. They make it all about the other person and forget that divine union with another is actually the external representation of their divine union within. If you are not showing up for yourself and honouring yourself, how can you do so for another? You cannot. More often, when one feels they are 'honouring' their partner, it is done with expectation. And when those expectations are not met, they feel resentment.

The commitment to self is where divine union begins. All that you would ever wish for in a relationship, must first be present within yourself. If you want a partner who honours you and treats you with love and respect, you must treat yourself in this way first. If you want a relationship with laughter, adventure and joy, you must first create that for yourself. If you want free, connected and 'out-of-this-world' sexual expression, you must first know how to cultivate this through your own connection to your body.

Your partner is not there to fulfil anything for you or plug any holes within. Your partner is there to augment all that you wish and all that you have already created for yourself. Together, you can share the magnificence of being two expressions of The All – two master creators of your own experience. You can marvel and delight in each other's differences, bringing greater expansion to your experiences. You can delight and find comfort in your similarities, experiencing the sense of 'home' that comes in seeing The All in another just as you see it in yourself. You can amplify all that you thought was possible, combining the power of the Rainbow Frequency in each of you. And you can allow the highest expression to unfold with complete non-attachment to outcome.

This is the ultimate expression of divine union with another. It is bringing the divine love essence of The All, onto your plane. It is amplifying this divine love, the Rainbow Frequency. It is the return of Earth to paradise through paradise within.

Bringing it back to divine union within, how does one embody this?

First, we wish to remind you that there is nothing you lack. Although you may need to connect with others for help and support with remembering, no other person or being can give you the answers. This tendency has long been a biproduct of the experiment in separation and, further, the Reign of Darkness, that caused all to forget they were the Rainbow Frequency. In this way, a single fragment of a Rainbow Unified Self felt it was incomplete. In one way this is true, for you are but one fragment of your Rainbow Unified Self, having an experience in separation in time and space. But, in your most complete form as your Rainbow Self, you exist outside of time and space. You are infinite, genderless and have a light body rather than a more dense physical form.

For this reason, it makes sense that each being across the multiverse might feel that something is missing. They might look beyond themselves for completion, such as with a partner, family, community or, in some cases, addiction.

However, this is not so. Yes, you are but one fragment of your Rainbow Self. But you are not 'incomplete'. Every fragment *is* the All-essence. Every fragment is constructed purely of the Rainbow Frequency. And through the Rainbow Frequency – your core essence of divine love – you have access to all that is. You have access to all of your other fragments, many of which you would call 'higher selves', 'past lives', 'angels', 'Gods' and 'Goddesses'. You have access to the core source. You know that all is love and love is all. And you are connected to everything, for all is one. Everything you see and even what you do not, is an expression of The All. The Rainbow Frequency runs through everything. So, there is nothing you lack. There is no disconnection. This is but an illusion.

In this way, the desire for another to 'complete' you or validate you or make you feel safe, is what you would call 'unhealthy'. This belief or desire is rooted in the illusion of separation. And it is why so many relationships, of all kinds, fail. Some put unnecessary pressure and significance on the approval of their parents and acceptance from their siblings. Some feel their partners are not giving them all that they need. Some feel they need to gain more stature or recognition within their communities.

Honouring yourself and surrounding yourself with relationships that honour, encourage, support and inspire you is important. Yet, this is different to trying to derive something from a relationship, such as validation, a sense of safety, recognition, acceptance and so on.

Every other human, like you, is a fragment of their Rainbow Unified Self having an experience in the experiment of separation. Yes, you chose to be human and allow yourself to have the fullness of that experience. But do not over-labour the human labels. Perhaps someone is your mother, father, sister, friend, boss, employee and so on. There are so many labels and, because of the way your society has been formed, each label comes with expectations.

If one does not meet the expectations of their role, you may consider them a 'bad mother' or a 'bad boss'. Yet, every other being is simply navigating their experience in separation. They are trying to find their way back to wholeness, back to the remembering that all is love and love is all.

Although you have agreed to meet certain souls through certain dynamics, such as being related, we invite you to release attachment. No one owes you anything. For there is nothing you need or lack. This is part of the illusion.

The way to bring out the best in all your relationships is to radiate at your best. Your greatest service to others and to the world is to commit to yourself. Heal past hurts. Release what is not yours. Re-embody all that you are at your essence. Radiate the Rainbow Frequency of divine love. Live your life through this embodiment.

When you do so, you realise that attachment and expectation are but traps of the human ego to hold you back. When you release these and come into cosmic love, you do not 'expect' anything from anyone. You love from a truly unconditional space. Although, we do wish to call out a distinction between unconditional love and being what you would call a 'doormat'. Your sovereignty is key. You can love unconditionally while still holding loving boundaries, saying 'no' when needed and remaining true to yourself.

So, the first priority is love for yourself. For how can you love 'God' or any other being and not love yourself? You are 'God'. You are The All, as is every other living thing. When you remember this, there is nothing to judge or blame. Yes, you will feel the human emotions. But in being present with them and releasing them rather than pushing them down, you pass through to the other side. As we have shared previously, always underneath grief or hate, you will find divine love.

When you come into your own embodiment of yourself as the Rainbow Frequency of divine love, you exude this frequency. And all of your relationships will shift around you. Some may drop away for they find the beauty and remembering too much at this point in their journeys. Other relationships will grow and expand and evolve in the most beautiful way. And new ones will form. You will become like the sun, shining on all of the delicate flower buds around you. In your presence, the presence of The All embodied, these buds will unfold and open into their full glory.

So, you see, when you are whole within yourself, you do not need anything from those around you. Yes, you will share and teach and support and inspire each other. But this is co-creation, which is very different to using another to fill a hole within yourself. And you can imagine that when two empowered beings like this come together in divine union, the results are nothing short of magical.

This is why the commitment to yourself and your divine union within is the most important promise you will ever make. It is how you achieve your purpose in life. For the purpose of all life across the multiverse is to remember. It is to re-embody your divine love essence, the Rainbow Frequency. It is to remember that you are The All, as is every other thing. And it is to emanate divine love which, by its frequency, will awaken divine love in all it touches.

Section 4

DIVINE UNION WITH ANOTHER

Raphael intertwined his fingers with mine. The black velvet of his skin was so beautiful against my milky complexion. He leaned over and kissed me, letting his lips linger. Then he kissed me again, wrapping his arm around my back and pulling me closer.

"I could just kiss you forever. It's like your lips are pure magic. You are magic." He laughed and scratched his head. "Oh, man. I never knew sex could feel like this. I never even knew a kiss could feel like this!"

He jumped out of bed and went to the kitchen to pour a glass of water for each of us. I watched as he crossed the room. The star-speckled Andean sky formed an other-worldly backdrop. It was only a studio apartment, but the floor-to-ceiling windows and glass door to the balcony made it seem twice as big.

Raphael handed me a glass and I sat up to drink it, holding the blankets against my naked body. It felt surreal, as though I were watching myself in a movie scene. Where had this man come from? He wasn't part of my original timeline. Yet there was no denying that our connection was divine union. And our intimacy was sacred. That reminded me of something.

"Hey, we need to be extra careful," I said. "I saw a baby hanging around above your head. We need to make sure we don't give it any opportunity to come through."

"Really? Ok. Although, I can think of worse things than having a baby with you." Raphael stroked the hair off my face and kissed my forehead.

I eased myself down and rested my head on the pillow. It was strange. We had only known each other for seven weeks and been a couple for two weeks. But Raphael acted as though it had been years. To him it was a given that we were going to spend the rest of our lives together.

Raphael traced his fingertips over the back of my hand and wrist. "Do you know that I knew you were coming?"

I gave him a puzzled look.

"I could have got out. The people staying in the other apartments left on one of the repatriation flights. But my guides told me to stay. I didn't know what I was waiting for. But I had a feeling it was a woman. Weeks and weeks passed. And I started to wonder if I had made a mistake."

He paused and looked deeply into my eyes.

"One day, the landlady told me a woman was moving into the apartment above me. I knew 'she' was the one – the reason I had to wait behind. I mean, come on? Who moves in the middle of a lockdown? It had to be!"

He cleared his throat, embarrassed. "I tried to catch a glimpse of you the day you moved in. I heard you on the stairs and opened the door a crack. All I saw was your shoulder and the back of your head, but my heart skipped a beat. It was like I recognised you.

"The next day I saw your huge shoes outside your door and I thought, 'Oh, good. She's tall like me.'" Raphael laughed and playfully wrestled me into a bear hug. He smothered my neck with little kisses, then rested his head on my chest.

It was incredible. Such divine weaving. Yet, I didn't quite know what to make of it. Lockdown time wasn't like normal time. Yet, that didn't mean I wanted to rush. This relationship had come out of nowhere. The magic was undeniable. But the whole thing felt like a lot.

Raphael rolled onto his back and the drowsiness of sleep washed over his face. There was no doubt that this man was special. What we were sharing was more pure than anything I had known. And I was open to seeing where it took us.

A few days later we had a ceremony day. The military lockdown seemed to have no end in sight. Police were guarding the nearby park. Every night the soles of my feet ached and burned. It felt like rockets coming out of them. It had been three months of doing powerful multidimensional work and channelling, with no access to the earth in order to ground. I had taken to rubbing frankincense and myrrh oils onto the soles of my feet. But I had to ration. Who knew how much longer this insanity would last? And there was nowhere to buy anything other than food and medical supplies.

So, we had decided to sit in ceremony with the grandfather medicine. A dear Wachumera, Ava, had a wonderful ceremonial house by the Temple of the Moon. There was no way to walk there without being fined or arrested. But one of her sons had brought a bottle of medicine to a nearby street where I had waited by a pharmacy. If I had been questioned, I would have said I needed to buy feminine products.

After opening sacred space and offering our gratitude and prayers of intention, we drank the medicine. Before long, the grandfather was sharing his wisdom with us. My intention was to receive whatever was needed to bring through the second book about divine union and sacred sexuality in its purest and highest expression.

In the early afternoon, while Raphael was on the balcony, I was suddenly overcome with the sensation of orgasm. Thanks to the channellings, I knew it was not about climax. It was the state of orgasm – becoming one with my Rainbow Frequency and experiencing myself as The All. For an hour or more, I walked around in this frequency, pausing every now and then to write in my journal. It was breathtaking.

Then the feeling intensified to the point where I could no longer stand. I lowered myself onto the bed. Breathing deeply, I undulated my body so I could hold the energy. Then something happened. It felt as though shooting stars, or more – an entire universe, was entering my womb. It was more powerful than anything I had ever felt. I groaned as the energy rushed in.

"You ok?" I heard Raphael ask from the balcony door.

"Yes," I said breathlessly. "It's the new codes. For the book. They're huge. Oh my God."

He sat on the couch to give me space and I stayed with the process. Each time I thought I had reached the maximum I could hold, the energy amplified. It was complete bliss. It was all of the cosmos and the stars and the wisdom.

My back arched and my yoni throbbed. My hands and feet were vibrating. It felt as though I were about to dematerialise.

"Raphael?"

"What do you need?"

"I can't hold it. It's too much. I need the masculine energy to balance it. I need you inside me. Not to have sex. Just to be in union of the feminine and masculine in that way."

Quietly and reverently, he did as I asked. We didn't move. He just held me. And my body and spirit exploded into cosmic expansion. I didn't know where I ended and the cosmos began. I was all of it. It was all within my womb. Raphael was both inside me and holding me. He felt like my only anchor to the Earth plane.

Minutes or hours passed. Time had no place in this sacred embodiment. Once all of the codes had settled, I let Raphael know. With a gentle kiss on my forehead, he went back to the balcony. He was silent but I knew he had felt the magnitude of what we had just experienced. I had known the book was going to be big. Already I had felt the power and activation in the channellings. But now I knew this book was going to literally change the world. Our perception of love and sex was so small and distorted compared to the actuality. The words weren't there yet. But the codes had landed.

With my hands on my womb, I let out a huge sigh. I was exhausted. I shook my head in wonder. Before I could integrate, I felt the next wave of medicine rise. The grandfather had more to share with me. Our journey was not yet done.

* * *

"When you are calling divine union into your life, it is not about calling 'the one' or a specific partner. It is about calling the essence of this sacred interplay and co-creation. Divine union is the container. The journey… Divine union is the way two people show up for themselves and each other, and embark on a deep, loving and powerful journey together."

Releasing spiritual labels

As we have shared, two can enter divine union already embodied in their wholeness, or still on the journey back to wholeness. In your time, the second is the more common. In 'The Rainbow Tablets: Journey back to wholeness', we went into detail about soul contracts. We also shared a very grounded approach to entering divine union. As you already have this base, we can now explore divine union on a deeper level.

Many wonder how they can find their 'soul mate' or 'the one'. You are in a period now where it is not only possible to live your highest timeline, but to exceed your original blueprint. Some, like the Channel, are choosing to jump up a number of timelines. This means that, in a way, they are living multiple lifetimes in the one lifetime. The Channel experiences this as folding time – bringing the future to the present.

Is it not wondrous that you are on Earth during a time of such incredible possibility? And this means that the old notions of one designated divine union partner no longer apply.

The highest purpose of twin flames is not to come together and be in lasting divine union. That may be the outcome, and it is wonderful. But the highest purpose is actually to activate the codes within each other. Coming together, no matter how briefly, activates deep remembering and catapults those who are ready onto their paths of highest service. Remember also that a 'romantic' connection is only one form twin flames can take. They can also incarnate as parents and children, friends, siblings or even share across interdimensional planes where one is incarnated and the other is not.

So, what about soul mates? We do not wish to use this term as it has been greatly misunderstood on Earth. All we wish to say is that there is not only one person who would fit the human idea of 'soul mate'. What is more 'soul mates' can also come in the form of close friends, children and so on.

Here we are starting to shatter the illusions for you. Many hold onto these notions tightly and it prevents them from calling in and receiving their highest divine union partner. What if you were to drop the spiritual labels? With that, you could drop the expectations.

What if you were to bring it back to truth, which is that each and every other being is an expression of The All? And what if you were to meet and connect with others based on who they were rather than what you thought they might be?

A great affliction facing many is that they ignore the embodiment of the person before them and focus on the potential. They see that this person – this 'twin flame' or 'soul mate' or 'the one' – has great beauty at their essence. Yet, this is true for every being. Even those who have committed the most heinous acts are still The All at their essence. The have just drifted into such deep separation and unhealed trauma that they have become encompassed by the dark side of duality.

It is not about what a person has the potential to be. Rather, it is about who they are. This does not mean they need to be perfect. Most likely, your partner or future partner will have things to work on and areas of growth. But it is about how they approach this. Are they abusive or manipulative, using projection and gaslighting to escape self-responsibility? Or are they self-aware and committed to being the best version of themselves?

To truly attract and choose the highest divine union for yourself, you must cast away the labels and expectations and allow yourself to be present. Get to know the person as they are. Observe their actions more than their words. Anyone can portray themselves in a certain way, but what does their embodiment tell you?

In the first manuscript we shared a great deal about ego death. In particular, we explored the need to release expectation and attachment. This is because expectation and attachment are ploys of the ego. They prevent you from seeing truth and living in flow. And they create a controlling energy dynamic. No doubt you have felt this when someone has placed expectations upon you. It may feel that they are not seeing you or not willing to get to know the real you. It may feel that they are trying to change you or make you fit a certain ideal. Likewise, attachment brings a suffocating and unhealthy dynamic. It emerges when one is not in flow or trust with the multiverse. So, they feel they need to hold onto something or someone. This inevitably drives the thing or person away.

Both of these traits are toxic in relationships. This is why we invite you now to let go of the labels, because labels carry expectations. And they may drive you to attach to a person because you think they are your 'one chance' at love and lasting union.

Rather, open yourself to the ever-flowing abundance of love and possibilities that the multiverse has to offer. Now that you can reach and exceed your intended highest timelines in one lifetime, it opens so many more possibilities. Perhaps your divine union partner will be one of the intended ones for this lifetime. Maybe it will be someone from a future timeline. Or it could be someone new altogether.

Also remember that divine union does not have to mean 'forever'. Divine union refers to the frequency of the relationship and the embodiment of the two. While some divine unions may last decades, others may be for a shorter period. That does not make them 'wrong' or mean the divine union 'failed'. Provided the relationship comes to an end respectfully and in truth, it just means that the two have gone as far as they can together. In order to move forward on their highest paths, the two may be called in different directions.

It is worth, at this point, mentioning the label of 'marriage'. Being in trust and allowing a divine union to flourish in its most true form does not mean you cannot get married. However, it does call for a reframing of what marriage means. This should be a commitment of intention and an honouring of the love. But it cannot be seen as a prison or obligation. If one knows in their heart and truth that their divine union has come to an end, staying would only lower the frequency (and highest expression) of both. It would create tension and resentment. And this can lead to infidelity, depression, anger and more.

Yet, many stay in these situations because they feel an obligation. Perhaps they do not want to disappoint their parents or their partner's parents. Maybe they feel the pressure of religious projections. Or they could feel that staying together even when the love is gone is best for the children.

You cannot walk your highest path and be the embodiment of The All if you are trying to live up to other's expectations. Just as the ego death requires you to release your expectations of others, you must also free yourself of the expectations placed upon you. It is not your role to please anyone else. You can only be responsible for acting with truth and integrity. You are not responsible for how others receive that. Their projections are part of their own healing journey. Why would someone be so invested in another's life? Why would someone feel they have the right to judge another? Because they are in separation within themselves. They are disconnected from their own divine love essence. That is theirs to heal, not yours to suffer.

Living outside of truth and connection is never the best for anyone. For example, children pick up on tensions and may form distorted views about how married couples treat each other. Or they might adopt a belief that relationships only bring fighting and unhappiness. Is it not better for children to see their parents happy and enjoying life?

When a divine union is dissolved with respect, most likely there will still be feelings of grief or hurt. But there is no terrible act needing to be healed. There is no cheating, or years of abuse or poor treatment. Therefore, there is no resentment. The two can move through the grief and let go. And they can then move forward amicably, providing wonderful examples for the children and showing them that it is ok to honour their truth.

When you trust and let go of forcing an outcome, you allow the greatest magic and alignment to present itself. And the first step to allowing this greater magic is letting go of the labels and expectations.

Practical ways to attract divine union

Divine union with another is not something that just happens. It is a conscious co-creation. Everything that you attract or create in your life is responding to your frequency. So, there are practical steps you can take to raise your vibration to match and attract that of divine union.

If you are already in a relationship, the embodiments below will elevate you. This means you can show up for your relationship in a more whole and conscious way. From there, your partner might also choose to elevate themselves. And you could discover that your relationship becomes so much more. Or, if your partner does not wish to grow, you may find that you have gone as far as you can with that partnership. This possibility may seem daunting. But you should never hold yourself back out of fear or attachment. Trust the universe to hold and guide you, and all will unfold for your highest good.

Let us share with you now some ways you can align your frequency to that of divine union.

1. Know your truth and centre

It is easy to lose yourself when you start to connect with someone. When you are not centred and grounded within your own energy field, you can get pulled into the other's programs or limiting beliefs. This can result in unbalanced dynamics of control, manipulation, energetic vampirism, co-dependency, and so on. These are the dynamics of lower-frequency egoic love.

In divine union with another, each partner knows that their sense of wholeness comes from within. Although you may not have fully achieved that yet, you are committed to that path. And you are not looking to use your partner to plug any void within yourself. Likewise, you are not looking for a partner who wishes to sustain themselves with your energy.

It is in this truth that you find your grounding. Your embodiment of your divine masculine within holds a safe container for you. Therefore, you are not open to being pulled into another's limiting beliefs or programs. And you are not willing to sacrifice what you know to be in alignment with your soul just so you can hold onto another out of fear. So, if something is against what you know to be your highest path, you are strong enough to place loving boundaries and, if necessary, walk away rather than deny your truth.

This is a choice the Channel herself had to make. From her early teens, she was confused by the way 'love' and 'sex' were expressed on Earth. She had a deep remembering of divine union and sex as sacred. And she committed to a path of remembering, re-embodying and sharing this gift with the world. Yet, like many, she made trade-offs along the way. Friends told her she was too idealistic and would never find a partner. So, she tried to date the 'normal' way. This only brought her pain and unhappiness.

As an adult, the Channel met her counterpart. She had not known what that was before they met, and the power of it took her by surprise. He had long been ensnared in the parasitical programs, which he hid from her. After almost a year together, the Channel's counterpart issued her an ultimatum. No matter how much she had wanted to walk forward with him, she knew she could not step into the distortions in order to do so. It was painful to leave. But she knew the pain of living out of alignment would be far worse.

The Channel's greatest commitment – even greater than her cosmic vow to her counterpart – was to The All. And she knew that was much bigger than this one relationship. It was not just a commitment to her highest service. It was a commitment to herself and to every other being. Because every being, everything in existence, is the expression of The All. And she could not turn her back on something so pure and cosmic in order to follow the lower programs she had come to break.

This is what we mean by knowing your truth and centre. At your essence, you are The All. You are divine love. No matter how much the lower programs may try to derail you, if you are grounded in your centre, you will always choose to honour the cosmic wisdom and remembering you hold within. And the multiverse will rush to support your highest service.

2. Be clear about your intention

The multiverse responds to your frequency and intention. There are no limitations. The underlying principle of the entire multiverse is co-creation. This experiment in separation was for The All to experience itself. And the fabric of co-creation is the Arraya pure abundance consciousness, which we share through the Channel as the Lyran Golden Abundance Codes. The Arraya is the infinite ever-flowing abundance of all that is. At the point of the creation of the multiverse, you gave a golden aspect of your consciousness to form the Arraya. So did every other being in existence. In this way, the Arraya is the consciousness of all that are.

How does this relate to intention? You are co-creating at levels beyond your wildest imaginings. This is far greater than what has been considered as 'manifesting'. You are not just able to create as the creator force. You are also part of the fabric of the ever-flowing and infinite co-creation.

This is why we invite you to be conscious in your co-creation. Your intention is one of the ways that you connect with the Arraya and weave your magic into being. Intention must be pure and free of limitations. This means you cannot set an intention of being with a specific person or making a particular relationship work. Attachment to outcome denies the multiverse use of the full magic and majesty available. And attachment and expectation are rooted in ego. We keep repeating this because we wish you to comprehend how much this limits you.

Rather, let your intention be focused on what you desire, free of outcome or form. For example, you may want a divine union where you are each free to follow your own service and dreams. One where you encourage and lift each other. One where there is honesty, faithfulness and laughter. One where there is adventure yet stability.

Be clear about the sort of union you desire. What you feel will align with your truth and empower you to flourish. Then let the multiverse and the Arraya bring you the highest possibility. You do not need to try to list the person's characteristics, age, location or whether or not they have children.

If you are clear and pure in your intention of what you wish to step into, the multiverse will respond. Because the Arraya is the infinite abundance of co-creation. And a golden aspect of your consciousness is part of the Arraya. In this way, *you* are the infinite pure abundance consciousness. So, when your intentions are pure and open to the greatest magic of the multiverse, you are creating as the creator force – the ultimate fabric of co-creation.

We know this is a big concept. In fact, it is an entire manuscript of its own. But we wish to help you start to align with the cosmic nature of yourself as a creator. This will empower you to transcend any societal perceptions you may have adopted about age, timing, appearance, circumstances and more. As we have said, there are no limitations. The power of co-creation is infinite. And your intention aligns you to the frequency of what you are attracting.

3. Be loving and open in your body

You are a multidimensional being. Right now, you are having a physical incarnation. This means that you and your body are a team. It is the vessel to carry you through this lifetime. It is there to support you in all that you desire. Yet, if the frequency of your body does not match the frequency of your intention, it is much harder for the multiverse to deliver what you desire. Remember that everything is made of frequency. In order to attract what you want, you must match that frequency – emotionally, mentally, spiritually, energetically and physically.

As you prepare for divine union, connect more deeply with your body. Let it talk to you. It has its own intelligence and can communicate with you if you listen. Where are you stiff, in pain, uncomfortable and so on? These are the places where you are holding energetic blockages or trauma. Do the work to clear them. Your body will tell you how. It might be something your heart is guiding you towards. Or it might be something you are aware of but resisting.

This is because the ego resists change and pain. Releasing trauma and stepping into growth scares the ego. But it is a short-term pain of release in order to liberate yourself. Real pain is holding on and suffering. It is denying yourself what your heart desires because your frequency cannot allow it to come towards you. Real pain is developing chronic illness or disease because the trauma and energy blocks have festered within your body. Do not let the ego fool you. Resistance is often a sign of what is needed in order to heal.

Also, as you prepare for divine union, actively bring yourself into greater love and acceptance of your body. It is a miraculous vessel! Appreciate it. Notice if you are speaking unkindly to it or criticising it. Would you talk to your best friend in that way? Your body is the best friend you will ever have. It is the only thing in physical form that will be with you your entire life. You cannot achieve anything on the Earth plane without your body. So, treat it like your best friend. Celebrate it. Love and cherish it. Tell it how much you appreciate it.

If there are things you wish to change about your body, dig a little deeper. For example, if you wish to have cosmetic surgery, what is beneath that? Many who have surgery to fix what they 'hate' about their bodies, come to regret that decision or even reverse it once they awaken spiritually. Why? Because they realise it was never about their body in the first place. Perhaps it was a fear of rejection due to not feeling accepted by their family or peers at school. Maybe it was a sense of unworthiness resulting from earlier abuse or trauma. In many instances, having to constantly see the results of the surgery after they have awoken, reminds them of a less happy, less loving and less accepting version of themselves.

We are not saying that surgery is never the right option. We are just bringing to your awareness that commercialised and distorted versions of 'perfection' are yet more of the disempowerment programs. Rather than feeling judgemental about your physical appearance, ask what it is that needs to be healed and loved.

That said, making healthy and loving changes to nourish your body can boost your energy, vitality and overall mood. Be sure to look at how you support your body. How clean and healthy is your diet? Would your body benefit from supplements or alternative therapies? What are your exercise and movement practices? How is your breathing and relationship with breath? Do you give yourself enough rest and rejuvenation? Small changes or fresh patterns can make a huge difference to how you feel in your body.

What is more, addictions or self-sabotage often play out through the relationship with the body. Be honest with yourself and make changes where needed. If you struggle to do this alone, find a practitioner to help. This is why they are there. You do not need to do it all alone and there is no shame in accepting help to make positive changes.

Finally, how do you feel sexually within your body? We will delve into this more deeply in the section about preparing for sacred sexuality. But let us seed the idea here. Do you feel sexy? Confident? Playful? Or do you feel embarrassed? Ashamed? Awkward?

Whatever the answer, can you love your body more? Can you celebrate it and introduce something that makes you feel more confident? This could be anything from a fragrance, such as essential oils, to new underwear or clothing. You could even spoil your body with something like a new workout routine, massage, sauna, float tank or even a rich moisturiser. And, of course, you can work with a more sensual and connected self-pleasure practice.

If your body is not open to receiving a divine union partner with whom you can explore sacred sexuality, then your frequency will not be aligned to attracting this. Stepping into sacred sexuality is something you can begin by yourself. Your relationship with your body, your own sexual expression and your senses will assist with this. We will share more about this later.

4. Clear chords and old sexual energy

Just as your physical body needs to be in alignment of frequency, so do your emotional, mental, spiritual and energetic bodies.

We shared about clearing old chords and ties in the last manuscript. Let us just briefly revisit this. There are a number of energetic processes for checking your etheric body for any hooks, chords, syphons and so on. If you are not familiar yet with how to do this for yourself, you can seek the assistance of a practitioner.

It is highly likely that you will have multiple sexual partners in your lifetime. This does not mean you are out of alignment with divine union and sacred sexuality. Divine union does not mean it has to last forever. Divine union is the state and frequency of the relationship. When two take a journey together in this frequency, it could be for the rest of their lives, just a few years or even a few months. The purity of the connection is not determined by the time. Part of divine union is always lifting and honouring each other. If two reach a point where journeying together is no longer in alignment with the highest path of one or both, parting ways might be the best way to honour each other.

What is more, in your time on Earth it is almost impossible to step straight into a high expression of sexuality. You are the ones who are breaking the old sex distortion programs. As with most of the programs you came to dismantle, you may enter the program on some level. There is no shame in this. Healing and remembering is a process. Just because you may have made one or many choices that were far from divine union and sacred sexuality, does not mean there is anything 'wrong' with you. Nor does it mean that, because you have taken on that energy, that you are now somehow excluded from stepping into sacred sexuality.

This is the Return to Unification. The Great Remembering and Great Awakening. You have the power to alchemise every experience you have had in your life, whether it came by choice or by circumstance. You can turn trauma into healing and enlightenment. You can turn 'mistakes' into lessons and remembering. You are sovereign and the choices you make in every now moment are what shape your path, not the experiences of your past.

It is important to clear the energy of past lovers or sexual experiences from your body and energetic field. You can take the growth with you, but you do not want to be tied to that person or old dynamic. There are so many ways to clear this energy. For women, it could include yoni eggs and womb work. For all genders, it could include cleansing practices such as the Temazcal (sweat lodge), Vision Quest, plant medicine, drumming, movement, multidimensional healing, and so on.

It is also necessary to release grudges and grief. If you are holding onto negative emotions, you are creating a pathway for that person to connect back into your energetic field. Or you might even be attaching to theirs. To call in a divine union partner who is aligned with what you desire, you must create the space for them to enter. If your other bodies are tied up with negative emotions or emotional attachments, the space is too crowded.

This means that you must be present with the work to release old relationships or traumas. Heal the hurts. If they need to come out through tears or safe expressions of anger, such as screaming underwater, jumping around and shaking the body or punching a boxing bag, give yourself permission. Release this emotion and residual energy as a witness, not a participant. Allow it to pass through you. The idea is to let go, not re-engage. If you become a participant, you will re-attach to the trauma and pain. Not only will you re-live it, but you will perpetuate it.

What is done is done. The only way forward is through healing and forgiveness. Forgiveness is not about condoning the actions of the other person. It is about liberating yourself. While you hold a grudge, anger, betrayal or distrust, you continue giving that person your power. The moment has passed. Yet, your unhealed feelings will keep you caught in re-living that reality each and every day.

You are not a victim. This is one of the dynamics of the wounded feminine. You are also not vengeful. This is an expression of the wounded masculine.

Every experience you have is an opportunity to come into more of your truth and sovereignty. We know this may be hard to believe if you have suffered at the hands of another. But, beneath anger is grief. Grief is ultimately the feeling of separation. Whether it is grief that a partner crossed over, grief that someone betrayed you, or grief about a heinous act. Essentially, anything that brings you to the point of grief is reconnecting you with the core wound of separation. It is the sense of feeling disconnected and cut off from source – The All. It is the sense or fear of being unsovereign, unsafe, unloved and not whole.

Liberation and truth lie on the other side of grief. If you can pass through the grief, which often feels like being cracked open, you will arrive at cosmic love. You will arrive at a greater understanding of sovereignty, safety, love and wholeness – realising that you hold them all within. And, yes, it is a process. It comes from presence and your own embodiment. It comes from shedding all that you are not, in order to rediscover all that you truly are. We say this a lot, because this is what the journey back to wholeness is all about.

You are not your experiences. But you can learn and grow from them. You cannot undo them. But you can heal and release them. So, we invite you to lean into the healing rather than run from it. Be present and patient and compassionate with yourself. Seek assistance. You do not need to do it alone. If you do not know where to start, we have shared many tools and healing through the Channel's courses and offerings. So, you may wish to visit her website. Or, if you feel you need more conventional support such as counselling, seek it out. The main thing is to start.

Be honest with yourself about where you are holding on. For example, the Channel's counterpart owed her a large sum of money. She knew she would probably never receive it. But there was part of her that was hoping he would step into integrity. As the years passed, her hope turned to anger and resentment. This was pulling down the Channel's frequency. In hoping for (attaching to) this outcome, she was still energetically and spiritually connected to her counterpart. She had done so much work to move through the grief and remove all chords. However, this one aspect of holding on meant she did not have the space to receive a higher divine union. When she realised this, she handed back the debt to the Arraya pure abundance consciousness and asked that it be returned to her by whatever divine means. Then she let go.

As a side note, once the Channel let go of the anger, it cleared the energy between her and her counterpart. There had been significant expenses during her father's transition. After he crossed over, the Channel was guided to ask her counterpart if he would consider paying back the money he owed her. This was only the second time in three years that she had asked. This time, there was no anger or attachment to outcome. After some open and loving discussions, her counterpart agreed and acted on it. Not all situations of clearing energetic ties will end in this way. The Channel had asked for the money to come back to her through divine means. These were the divine means that were chosen. And it also gave her counterpart a wonderful gift of growth and healing.

So, sometimes these chords and ties can be obvious. Other times they can be quite subtle and hidden. Take the time to clear, release, heal and liberate yourself. If you do end up in a new relationship before you are fully done with the work, keep going. Otherwise, these old chords and ties will block the fullness of your new union, and they may play out through insecurities, jealousy, distrust and so on. The more that you create space and return to your true essence, the more easily you will be able to foster a loving and flourishing divine union.

5. Be grounded in your practice

It is easy when you feel a deep connection with a new partner to get swept up in it. If you are not grounded with firm roots, you may find yourself wanting to spend every free moment with them. This can lead to cancelling or neglecting the activities that keep you in your highest frequency and divine connection. Perhaps you might stop exercising, seeing friends or meditating. Before long, you will have lost yourself and slipped down into an egoic form of love based on attachment and co-dependency.

It takes awareness and discipline to remain grounded as those strong currents of being enamoured with another wash over you. But it is necessary in order to move into divine union rather than lower forms of relationships that inevitably burn out. You are responsible for your sense of wholeness, not another. You are responsible for keeping your cup filled, not another.

To remain centred and grounded, you must be committed to yourself. This means being able to hold loving boundaries. Sometimes these will be with your partner. For example, when they want to see you, but you know that you need to place your time in an activity that will re-centre you. Other times, these boundaries will be with yourself.

Egoic love often centres around two people trying to fill up themselves from the other and the relationship. It inevitably becomes a power struggle and a dynamic of being 'disappointed' or 'let down' because the other is not living up to the unrealistic expectation placed upon them. Or it becomes a battle for control. These old dynamics are unhealthy and keep both parties disempowered. So, it stands to reason that you cannot enter divine union by falling into these patterns of old.

Divine union is about two whole people walking alongside each other. As you prepare for your divine union with another, take time to discover what makes you flourish. This could include regular exercise, meditation, time with friends and time in nature. We highly recommend a morning practice. In particular, you may wish to start and end your day with the Rainbow Pyramid sacred design we shared in the first manuscript. The first hour of your day sets your energy for all that you are co-creating and manifesting in that day. When you are single, the temptation is to roll over and hit snooze, or pick up your phone and scroll. When you are in a relationship, the temptation is to cuddle and take extra time with your partner. In this way, you see that there will always be distractions. It comes down to the commitment to yourself.

Through trial and error, you will discover what you need to keep feeling whole and grounded. It is not a passive process – especially in this time when the old corrupt structures are crumbling. There is much energetic debris and fear and confusion from the collective. So, wholeness is not something you attain and then forget about. It is an active process. It is something that needs to be cultivated and nourished. It can be attained and then lost. If you drop away your practices and get sucked back into the old programs, then you re-engage with the matrices and lower realities.

What is more, there is no finish line in your journey back to wholeness. That is the beauty of this grand adventure on Earth. There is always more to discover. More to remember. More gifts and passions to awaken. You are a master creator. This life has no limitations. When you are grounded and centred and open to continued expansion, you will be amazed at what comes forth. It will exceed your wildest dreams.

This is why your embodiment and grounding in your own practices are so important. It does not mean that you are rigid or inflexible. Your practices may shift as life pulses and evolves. This could be due to a new relationship, a new job or moving country. Everything is in divine flow. But it is the awareness of what you need and the commitment to cultivate that support for yourself, so you can feel whole and grounded. It is the promise to yourself to speak your truth and hold loving boundaries when needed, be it with yourself, a work place or a partner. And it is the presence and honesty to be constantly checking in with yourself. You will know when you start to feel 'off' or out of sorts. With presence, you can discover what you need and act on it, in order to feel more 'you' and aligned with your Rainbow Frequency of divine love.

6. Hold your divine union within

We will not go too deeply into this. There is a whole section about unifying the divine feminine and divine masculine in 'The Rainbow Tablets: Journey back to wholeness'. We have also shared more in this manuscript. But we do feel it is necessary to acknowledge again here.

Perhaps you have heard people say that their partner 'completes them'. This is one of the most ingrained mindsets of the disempowerment parasitical programs. The idea that you are but half and need another to complete you promotes energetic vampirism. In this dynamic, each will remain anchored in separation. At first, they will feel filled up by their partner. But, as time goes on, that gnawing sense of not being whole within will leave them feeling unfulfilled, like something is missing. So, they will try to draw more and more from their partner. They will drain each other and, in some cases, one or both may look outside the relationship as a way to gain more energy. Essentially, they will feed on each other until there is nothing more to take, then look for an energy source elsewhere.

Regardless of gender, you hold both the divine feminine and divine masculine within. Yet, due to life experiences, ancestral lineages, societal pressure and so on, you may have had more experience with the wounded and toxic forms of the feminine and masculine. A key part of your journey back to wholeness is healing these toxic forms and returning to the divine forms. In order to embody divine union with another, you must hold divine union within.

This means harmonising these divine energies within yourself. When one carries a deficiency or imbalance of one or both of these energies within, they will often look for a partner who holds what they do not. However, because they are holding the wounded forms within, they will usually attract a partner who is also holding wounded forms or distortions. On the off chance that they do attract a partner who holds the pure forms within, this partner will likely have to leave. For, they will not be able to sustain both themselves and the needs of the other person.

The only way to hold and nurture divine union with another, is to hold it within. This does not mean that you must be fully healed and whole prior to meeting a partner. This is a journey that can be taken together. But each must be committed to the process and responsible for their own process. Yes, each may hold space for the other and encourage them. But it is not about devolving into a low-frequency dynamic of victim and saviour.

So, as we shared in the first manuscript, "Use the divine feminine to explore ideas and invoke divine inspiration. And use the divine masculine to bring it to this plane. Allow your feminine to be compassionate and nurturing and your masculine to know when to place boundaries. You are both, so harness both. When they are brought into unity, this is the Rainbow Frequency."

7. Have other goals and passions

When two come together in egoic love union, they will often merge and become the collective noun. There is only 'we' and 'us'. They will not do anything without the other. There are couples who will not go out to dinner with friends or a movie if one of them is working, because they do not feel it is ok to have fun without their partner. There are couples who lose their individual interests when they come together and will only take part in activities that they both enjoy. No doubt at some point in your life you have seen either yourself or a friend 'lose themselves' in a relationship. While shared interests and experiences are wonderful, at the extreme it becomes co-dependency. That is, again, parasitical energy.

In divine union, each is fully engaged in life and following their highest path. They know that living their highest expression means connecting with what brings them joy. Joy is the heart's way of showing you what is in alignment with your core essence. To walk your highest path is to feel great expansion, joy and fulfilment. And anyone who is whole or on the path to wholeness within, wishes this for their partner.

Divine union is two people living their greatest expression who have chosen to walk alongside each other and share the journey. It can take many forms. Perhaps they are married with children. Maybe they are fully committed but do not feel the need for marriage. Or they could live in different countries yet make a more global lifestyle work.

There are no paradigms for a divine union relationship. Yes, it is the commitment of a sacred container between two people. But, as we have shared in the first manuscript, divine union is the ultimate freedom. It is free from the parasitical programs. It is free from ego and the need to wear masks to live up to an expectation. It is free from co-dependency and energetic control dynamics.

Each partner is fully authentic and able to fill up themselves. There is complete trust and the knowledge that sexual interaction with another would be much lower-frequency than the sacred sexuality within the divine union. Besides, infidelity is usually driven by a need one is not filling for themselves. A need to feel worthy, desirable, adventurous, and so on. In divine union, each partner is conscious of their needs and takes responsibility for any feelings that arise of not being fulfilled or whole.

We share this to illustrate that divine union is not limited by the constraints or expectations of the old programs. There is trust and commitment, and a removal of the unhealed aspects within that would drive a person to break the sacred container.

In this way, those in divine union can feel fully supported in following their own goals and passions. There is no fear that each having their own goals, passions and successes would somehow drive the two apart. There is no insecurity of being 'left behind', even if the pursuit of a goal or passion leads to some time apart in different states or countries.

In divine union, each takes great delight in seeing their partner soar. It is still possible that inferiority or lack of fulfilment could arise for one. But, in a conscious and sacred container, these shadow aspects are not projected onto the partner. The solution is not to try to hold back or tear down the partner to make oneself feel better. Rather, these shadow aspects become signposts for personal growth and open communication with their partner.

Each feeling fully supported to walk their highest path and service is one of the defining characteristics of divine union. It is also a powerful tool in preparing yourself for divine union with another. It is fine to desire union and be open to receiving it. Yet, if your core focus or most heart-felt goal is to find your divine union, the union is likely to fail. This is because you would be looking for the relationship to bring you fulfilment. No relationship can live up to that or withstand that kind of pressure.

Imagine that one's goal was to find their divine union, in the hope that they would then feel fulfilled. Happiness, joy and purpose can never be dependent on another person. So, what would be under the surface of such a desire? Perhaps there is loneliness, a desire to be accepted, or a need to feel safe. Maybe there is a sense of emptiness because they are not pursuing their true passion or feel they do not have direction in their life. These are wounds that need to be healed.

For a goal or passion to be aligned to your true Rainbow Frequency of divine love, it cannot be rooted in pain, lack or trauma. It should come from a call within your heart. This could be triggered by an activity that lights you up. Or it could be a sense of divine inspiration or remembering of why you came to Earth at this time.

Pursuing your passions helps you come into a fuller expression of who you are. And it takes the emphasis off 'needing' or 'longing for' a partner. Rather than trying to plug a hole with someone external, you are filling up yourself from within. You might say that you do not know your passion, goal or purpose. That is ok. Life is a journey of discovery. It is an unfolding. As the Channel likes to say, "Just follow the breadcrumbs."

If you feel the desire to learn a new language, do it. You do not need to have a trip or overseas move planned to justify it. If you want to learn an instrument or start painting, go for it. It does not mean you are committing to joining a band or holding an exhibition. Often these passions or soul calls unlock hidden aspects of yourself. You do not need to know the destination. Just allow the magic and mystery to be woven.

Or, if you have a burning desire to change profession entirely but do not have the skills or qualifications required, take the first step. Dreams and inspiration (divine feminine) exist in the etheric state. Everything is possible. But it only becomes so once you anchor the dream onto this plane through action (divine masculine). If you want your life to change or evolve, follow those whispers of the heart. It knows. It can guide you. And the more that you create your own fulfilment, the less you will look to someone else to fill you up. This empowers you to attract a union based on empowerment and divinity rather than need and co-dependency.

8. Trust in the divine unfolding

When a loving and sovereign desire to call divine union into your life comes from a place of wholeness, this frequency will attract one who is aligned. Trust in the divine unfolding. Many wish to meet 'the one' from an early age. This is why we started this section by asking you to release spiritual labels. Expectations only serve to sabotage relationships. Often one may be so desperate to find 'the one' that they believe every partner is that person. They may overlook many signs of misalignment and even accept mistreatment because the fantasy is more important than the reality. At the other end of the spectrum, one may be so focussed on meeting 'the one' that they find immediate fault with every potential relationship and sabotage any possibility. And there is a whole range of behaviours between these extremes.

This is why we invite you to release spiritual labels, expectations and attachments to outcome. These egoic traps are not aligned with the frequency of divine union. Also remember that not every divine union is forever. Sometimes there will be unions along the way that help each partner to grow and come further onto their highest path. These are not lesser forms of divine union just because they did not last a lifetime. And, sometimes, these shorter or mid-length divine unions are necessary to prepare for the longer-term divine union.

We summarise these points because we wish to invite you to be patient. Trust the divine flow. There is no rush. You do not need to force someone to become something they are not. Nor do you need to settle for someone who is not the right match for the frequency you are holding.

Divine union and sacred sexuality with another is a wonderful experience. But it is not the defining aspect of your experience on Earth. It is not, as your expression goes, "The be all and end all". You are a powerful multidimensional being on Earth during the Great Awakening. You are The All having an experience in separation. You are helping to restore Earth to paradise, which starts with paradise within. You are celebrating and embodying the Return to Unification. And you are rediscovering how to weave your creator force – the Rainbow Frequency – to create your highest reality and greatest service.

That is incredible! What a gift to be on Earth at this time. Perhaps you would like to share that journey with a sacred partnership. Yet, this is only one aspect of this incredible adventure on Earth. Trust in the timing. Be patient. But do not hold yourself back. Walk your highest path. Follow your greatest joy. Allow your heart to guide you. Co-create with others and continue expanding into more and more of your remembering. And if you prefer to walk some or all of your path without divine union with another, that is absolutely fine. It is your experience to choose and create.

When you are whole or moving into wholeness, you will feel more fulfilled. You will be in embodiment of divine union within and can practice sacred sexuality by yourself. And, when you are resonating at this frequency, you are more likely to attract a partner who can meet you. A partner who is in alignment with divine union and is not looking for you to complete them. So, be open to receiving your divine union partner if you desire one, but do not make it the focus. Allow the multiverse to work its magic.

Elevating an existing relationship

All that we have shared in this section can be embraced by those who are already in relationships. However, we know that there may be a burning question for some.

"Is it possible to elevate an existing relationship into divine union?"

The answer is, "Yes." This can be done if both partners are willing. And there are different ways for this willingness to arise. Allow us to illuminate some different pathways to divine union.

Conscious agreement

This is where both partners agree to take the journey together. This could be grounded through ceremony and intention. It is a commitment to show up for each other. More than that, it is a commitment to self. Each commits to self-awareness and responsibility of their behaviours, patterns and actions. And each is dedicated to coming into their highest embodiment and highest path. This starts by doing the work to shed all that they are not and uncover all that they truly are. But it also includes following the calls of the heart and soul. This could be through new hobbies, a new career, taking an existing profession to the next level, visiting sacred lands, and so on.

In order to come into divine union with another, each must come into divine union within. So, divine union cannot be reached by 'being in each other's pockets', as your expression goes. Yes, the two walk alongside each other and lift each other. But they must each be deeply in tune with what they need to release, heal, activate and awaken. The journey can be *taken* together but not *done* together.

Personal journey

Imagine a situation where one does not wish to evolve the relationship but the other, who is willing, does not feel ready to give up and leave. The one who is willing must be true to their own journey back to wholeness. They cannot hold themselves back for their partner. And they cannot force themselves to leave if that is not what feels aligned.

The personal journey will always deliver the highest outcome. When you commit to coming back to wholeness and being in your highest service, the multiverse will give you full support. Situations or realisations will arise to show you what you need to heal or release. Magic and blessings will flow forth. The journey will command a lot of presence and courage, but it will be more rewarding than anything you have known.

When only one partner in a relationship commits to their journey back to wholeness and highest service, most likely one of two things will happen. Perhaps the other partner will be touched and inspired by the higher frequencies and transformation they are witnessing. It may propel them onto their own journey. In this way, as one rises, it empowers and inspires the other to also rise. And they can take the journey to divine union together.

Or, the non-willing partner could feel triggered. They may decide to retreat further into their shadow aspects or denial. The chasm between the two will widen and the disconnection of the frequencies and intentions will become more apparent. In this dynamic, it will become clear to the partner doing the work that they cannot reach their highest expression while in this relationship. Most likely, the relationship will need to end.

These are some examples. However, like anything, the outcome is not pre-determined. It does not matter whether the two are dating, married, soul mates, twin flames or any other way relationships might be categorised. Nothing is guaranteed or pre-determined. And you are never bound to another. So, yes, it is possible for a relationship to be elevated into divine union. But, if one partner is not willing, the other who is, must follow their highest path. This will always lead them to their highest alignment, and the relationship will either evolve or drop away.

The essence of divine union

We have spoken much of the greater significance of divine union. Let us now take a moment to really summarise it in its purest and most tangible form.

Divine union is something that, first and foremost you hold within yourself. It is the harmony and unification of your divine feminine and divine masculine within, regardless of your gender.

79

Divine union with another is a sacred container and shared journey of two people in beautiful alignment. Each is either whole within or on their journey to wholeness within. They are not 'needing' anything from the other. Intimacy is created through each allowing themselves to be fully seen by the other, and to fully see the other. There are no expectations, attachments or projections. They show up for themselves and they show up for their partner. And the purpose of the union is to share the journey. To lift each other. To be the expression of divine love – The All. To witness the expression of The All in their partner. And to co-create as The All embodied, experiencing itself through another.

When you are calling divine union into your life, it is not about calling 'the one' or a specific partner. It is about calling the essence of this sacred interplay and co-creation. Divine union is the container. The journey. The way you honour, lift and love yourselves and each other through the union.

When you realise this, you can let go of all preconceived ideas. The person to join you in divine union could be of any race. They could live in your same area or a different country. They could work in a spiritual field or mainstream role. They could be a soul with whom you have had many lifetimes or a new connection.

So, we wish you to liberate any ideas that there is only one person in the entire world with whom you can experience divine union. As we have shared, timelines are changing. Twin flames, counterparts and soul mates are more than the limited notion you have been led to believe. And divine union is the way two people show up for themselves and each other, and embark on a deep, loving and powerful journey together.

Section 5

COSMIC DIVINITY OF GENDER AND SEX

The bathroom tiles were cold under my bare feet. Or perhaps it was me that was cold. It felt like time had stopped and I realised that I was holding my breath. The wet patch moved up the stick and the first red line instantly appeared. That was normal. They all had that. No biggie.

As the wet patch rose to the top of the section, a second faint pink line started to emerge. I waited. Maybe I was just seeing things. It was really faint. It could have been nothing. But it became darker and darker. Soon it matched the colour of the other line. Two lines. There were definitely two lines. I exhaled loudly and realised I must have been holding my breath again.

I picked up the stick and stared at it. Well, that was it. I was pregnant. Four weeks into our relationship. The day before my thirty-ninth birthday. The middle of a global meltdown. And I was pregnant.

Coming out of the bathroom, I held up the stick to Raphael. He sat bolt upright with wide eyes. "Is that..?"

"Yep."

I moved to the couch and sat down slowly. We looked at each other across the room and started to laugh.

"Wow." I said. Then laughed again.

Raphael cupped his cheeks in his hands, then brushed them off and shook his face. "Whoo. Whoa. Wow. We're having a baby!"

I moved to the bed and sat next to him. We looked at the bag of food and Raphael slowly unpacked it. Most restaurants had gone out of business. But a few had re-opened for takeaway now as the restrictions started to ease. While we were down the street buying the pregnancy test, we had taken the opportunity to get something to eat.

I picked up a french fry and nibbled it in slow motion. A baby. That was crazy. How had this even happened? I mean, I knew how it had happened. But how had it happened? We had been careful. I started to laugh again. So did Raphael. We looked at each other, then looked straight ahead. I picked up another french fry.

"I want you to know that I'll respect whatever you choose. But I am all in. Like, *all* in." Raphael held my hand and looked meaningfully into my eyes. Then he placed his hand on my belly and smiled.

"Shit."

It was all I could muster. The whole thing felt surreal. I had to be watching someone else's life unfold. I didn't even want children. But I had felt that if I ever fell pregnant by accident with the right person, I would embrace it. And now, here I was.

"I think I have to have it. I mean, it's happened for a reason. Right?"

I looked at Raphael, half-excited and half-bewildered. His face erupted into a huge smile. He grabbed my cheeks and kissed me.

"I'm going to be a dad!" His enthusiasm made me laugh. This was all so insane. But we were both in. All in.

The next day was my birthday and the first day out of lockdown. We bought some flowers and I took Raphael to one of my favourite spots. The Temple of the Moon. If we were going to accept this baby, we needed to do it right – through ceremony.

The climb was tough. Three and a half months of not being allowed outside to exercise had taken its toll. When we finally reached the top, Raphael stood dead still. He looked like he had seen a ghost. There were tears in his eyes.

"Are you ok?" I asked.

"Ah... Whoa." He shook his head. "Ok. Whoa. So, this is freaking me out. Remember that I told you the mountains near our house were really similar to the place my guides used to take me on the rainbow highway?"

I nodded.

"Well, this *is* the place. The exact place. This is it. Oh, man. I need a moment."

He walked off and sat on the seat at the Condor Temple. I hung back to give him space. A lot of time passed and I enjoyed the scratchy grass against my hands and feet after so long of only feeling cement and floorboards. Eventually, Raphael returned.

"Ok. I'm ready."

One by one, we entered the cave known as the Womb of Pachamama. We each offered a red rose and a prayer. Then we went in together and offered a white rose for the baby. We placed it between the two red roses and let this new soul know that it was welcome. Together, we emerged from the cave, stepping into the new.

That week, we visited a doctor. Everything was fine. The nausea had hit me hard though. The sight or thought of food made me want to vomit. All I wanted was laksa or baked beans. Neither existed in Cusco. But Raphael did everything he could to make it easier on me.

One day on the roof when I felt like I was going to throw up, Raphael looked at me with his mouth agape.

"Don't take this the wrong way, but because you're so sick you look 10 years older. And I've just realised something. The guide who brought me here to Peru via the rainbow highway was you! I said she looked like you because she was so much older. But now, seeing you like this, I realise it was you! We met on the astral plane a year and a half ago."

Later that afternoon, I went to the toilet. When I turned to flush, my heart froze. The water was red. I was bleeding. I couldn't lose the baby! We had only just adjusted to the idea of having it.

We jumped online and read that sometimes a little bleeding was normal. But it continued into the evening. I sent my doctor a photo. She said the pregnancy was at high risk and I needed to rest.

My heart was breaking. I was scared of losing the baby. And I was scared of the pain of miscarriage. I had only been pregnant once before, when I was 25. At six weeks I had miscarried and ended up in the emergency ward from the pain. Given the current context, going to the hospital wasn't possible. Whatever was going to happen, we were going to have to get through it on our own.

Raphael held me while we silently watched a movie. When it was over, he kissed me goodnight and said he was going to sleep downstairs in his room.

"What?" I asked in shock. "You can't! What if I miscarry? I will need you."

"You'll be fine. My back is hurting and I can feel it's about to go out. I need to get a good night's sleep. If you need me, just come down and wake me."

Panic took over. "Raphael, you don't understand. If I miscarry, it is going to be excruciating. I won't be able to walk down two flights of stairs. Please! I'm scared. I need you to stay with me."

He wouldn't budge. Our beautiful little bubble burst wide open. And when he closed my door behind him, I laid in bed feeling more alone than ever before.

Was this what it was going to be like? My whole life was about to change. I needed to know that when things got tough, my partner would be there. All of a sudden, the reality of the situation was right in front of me. We barely knew each other. If he couldn't put the threat of a painful and gut-wrenching miscarriage above his back pain, what did that mean for the rest of it?

Then it hit me. If this pregnancy did go ahead, there was a very real possibility I would be raising the child alone.

It was a long and emotional night. The next day I told Raphael how I had felt when he left me alone in such a vulnerable time. He didn't understand. He said he wanted to be able to look after me throughout the pregnancy, but couldn't do that if his back gave out. I shared that this made me concerned for the tough times ahead. He didn't want to talk about it. And in the afternoon, he threw his hands in the air and said, "I can't do this!" Then he walked out of my apartment.

My heart tore in two. I sobbed. Here I was, pregnant, single and on the other side of the world during in a global pandemic. How had our beautiful divine union ended up like this?

At least he had the option to move on from it all. But I still had a baby in my womb. My life felt like it had completely fallen off the tracks. So I called the only man I could truly trust. The only man who loved me unconditionally and had the purest heart of anyone I knew. The video call connected and I was greeted by a familiar smiling face. I let out a huge sob.

"Dad, I need your help."

* * *

"The remembering is returning… It starts with your own healing; your own embodiment. Every single being on Earth, regardless of their gender or sexual orientation, has the power to re-embody the highest sacred magic. They have the power to restore divine union and sacred sexuality to Earth."

Unravelling gender and sex distortions

What we are about to share may seem strange given the proliferation of gender classifications on your planet at this time. To understand the role of gender as divine expression, let us first highlight this journey as parallel to the multiverse's journey.

At the highest cosmic level, we started as our Rainbow Unified Selves. We were (and are) infinite beings outside of time and space with no gender, no physical form, no birth or death. When we agreed to the experiment in separation, each Rainbow Unified Self split into many fragments of itself. These fragments lived (and still live) in different times, dimensional planes, star systems and star races. The purpose of it all was to experience.

Now, we are all coming back to unification. All fragments are being called together into wholeness. All time and space are gently and lovingly collapsing as we come back to 'The Dimension' – a plane beyond time and space where All is one, all is love and love is all.

So, you see, when the purpose of it all is experience, there is no wrong. There is no judgement. Whether a fragment of a Rainbow Unified Self was a pure higher-dimensional being helping other beings, or it was a member of one of the star races that caused great harm during the cosmic wars, both are The All. Both are love. Because love is All. And this was a journey into the unknown into which we all embarked together.

Although this process of coming back to wholeness does involve healing and unplugging from all illusions and distortions, there is no judgement. We started as whole beings with no gender. Then, gender was created in its divine forms. It was part of the experience – a way to embody and more deeply experience the divine feminine and divine masculine. Over time, gender

88

became distorted, misunderstood and rejected. But you are now starting the journey back to the divine forms of gender. Beyond that, all in the entire multiverse will come back to one as the Rainbow Race. And gender will, once more, cease to exist.

When you look at it in this way, you can see there is no offence to be taken at the process. It has been like a huge journey around a circle. We began in wholeness. Then we devolved into deeper and deeper fragmentation. Now we are coming back to evolution and wholeness. All is divine. Because the purpose of it all was to experience.

So, we ask you to release the constriction of expectations and your current 'norms' around this topic. For we are sharing at much higher levels than the control dynamics and distortions playing out on Earth.

Those coming into divine union are the anchor points helping to restore the remembering – the full cosmic sovereignty and magic. These divine unions may be in mixed-gender unions, same-gender unions, or held within through solo practice. Each is bringing great healing and great service. Every beautiful being on Earth has the option to be the expression of the divine love essence – the Rainbow Frequency. This is not dependent on gender, sexual orientation or marital status. We will expand on this. But first, we need to take you on a journey.

In the beginning, when the experience in separation was created, time and space were formed. These were necessary to give shape to the experiment. Otherwise, each fragment would have been suspended in a pocket of infinity. And this experiment was never meant to last forever.

Because the purpose of this experiment was for The All to experience itself, gender was formed. The human bodies were designed as a key and a lock to reveal the great Rainbow Bridge back to The All. As we have shared, pure orgasm is a state of touching The All. It is a moment of transcending all separation, time and space, and being completely whole once more. This is why we will share about the role of becoming the orgasm and vibrating at the frequency of wholeness and bliss.

And so it was, in the beginning, that the cervix was the Rainbow Bridge within. The womb was the portal between dimensions – the way in which a soul could pass from the higher realms in order to incarnate on Earth. In this way, the womb also held the cosmic wisdom and magic. The Rainbow Bridge was activated when the 'key' – the penis – entered the cervix through divine union. With this coming together, the key unlocked the great magic and the two were able to weave using the fullness of their creator force. It was how the highest levels of sacred sexuality were activated.

As you know, during the great cosmic wars, certain star brothers and sisters who were more lost in the darker side of this experience in separation, interfered with Earth. They fed on the lower frequencies of fear, disconnection, loneliness, helplessness, conflict, and so on. We refer to them collectively as parasitical beings.

The parasitical beings knew that humans had direct access to The All through the embodiment of divine union and the practice of sacred sexuality. While this was so, these beings could never induce a state of fear, hopelessness and disconnection. And these lower-frequency states had become their food source, an addiction of sorts. So, they implanted programs onto Earth and into the human DNA to cut off the sacred connection. The most potent of these were the sex distortion programs.

Some of these beings incarnated on Earth to accelerate the spread of these programs. Sex became an act of base desires. This parasitical energy was like feasting on another, and was even used to pull in multiple participants, some willing and some not. It became intrinsically linked to ego, supported by the way this sticky web was spun into societal structures. And, to ensure that the sacred magic and remembering held in the womb was cut off, the divine feminine had to be suppressed and replaced by an oppressive and disempowering toxic masculine. For the divine masculine never would have dishonoured or harmed the divine feminine.

Sex became about power and status. The parasitical beings spread the distortions like a disease. And they used false light constructs to position it. In some areas, this seeped into culture as a man's right to take what he wanted from women. It even went so far as 'owning' or 'trading' women and children for sexual purposes. In other areas, it was positioned as 'free love', a program that has been present throughout history for longer than you could imagine. Its energy was like that of the leech – attaching, sucking life force, taking its fill. It was far removed from sacred emotional and spiritual connection between two. And as it spread like a virus, it bred more and more disconnection.

The control and power one felt from engaging in the sex distortions was like a drug. For a moment, it made them feel less of the hopelessness and disempowerment. They felt in control. They felt liberated. They felt filled up. And they wanted more. Yet, these very acts were taking them further and further from their divine cosmic truth and remembering.

At the societal level, the darkest and most vile acts a human could engage in formed a writhing underbelly. You know these now as rape, the sex industry, sex-trafficking and child-trafficking.

We do not wish to dwell on this further. It is just to illustrate the history. It was an inspired master plan – disconnect one from the greatest magic and expression of their creator force by inverting their direct avenue to access it. In this way, divine union and sacred sexuality were stolen from humanity. Sex became wrapped in sticky webs of parasitical energy. And this was seeded through societies at every level – from the darkest underbelly to the everyday approach to dating where pressures to 'put out' or 'score' reign.

To bring it back to gender, the rise of the distorted masculine and suppression of the divine feminine produced another inversion. The wounded feminine. For many centuries these two energies prevailed. But, as you have no doubt felt, as the false grids are being deconstructed, it has given space for the divine masculine and divine feminine to rise once more. We have already shared about this in 'The Rainbow Tablets: Journey back to wholeness'. Here we wish to delve a little deeper.

The distortions and parasitical energies turned gender into a tool for division and control. The breakdown of gender and the proliferation of sexual identity is nothing new. Most on Earth, regardless of their expression of gender or sexuality, are not engaging in sacred sexuality. This is because it is not reflected in societies and the remembering is only just starting to return. So, how can one embody something that has long been forgotten?

Whether a person identifies as heterosexual, homosexual or another sexual expression, they are being called to reject the parasitical paradigms. All are being called to unplug from the base and disempowering programs so they can reclaim their power. Many on Earth now – who are choosing all sorts of gender expressions and sexual orientations – have incarnated to be in great service. And part of embodying this service is through the restoration of divine union and sacred sexuality. But first we must share the history that led to this service being called in from the higher realms.

As the parasitical programs spread throughout societies and cultures like a disease, it birthed many forms of sexual distortions. Divine union was attacked by infidelity and polygamy. As time went on, this was further consumed by the rise of 'free sex' mentalities and trends such as 'open relationships'.

Indoctrination brought another dimension to suppressing sacred sexuality. In some doctrines, sex was labelled a sin or prohibited except under specific circumstances. Women were considered impure seductresses. They were blamed for man's inability to control his base desires. Historically this often led to death, such as the era of witch trials. While other doctrines still give way to heinous acts in your current time, such as women being stoned to death or mutilated so they can never feel pleasure.

In some cultures, divine union was (and still is) undermined by removing choice – meaning the heart could not lead. Often, in these arrangements, fidelity only applied to the women, while the men continued to engage with other sexual partners. Worse still, some of these transactional marriages took place between children and adults. And this was an accepted part of 'culture'.

So, you see how these distortions took on many forms and seeped into your societies and psyche. Divine union and sacred sexuality were all but forgotten. And the parasitical programs prevailed.

Without connection to and expression of divine union and sacred sexuality, humans forgot how to touch The All. They forgot that they were The All, as was every other being.

Even those who connected with sex as an act of love – an expression from the heart that then led the body – were still not able to reach the highest levels of sacred sexuality. Because the distortions were too deeply embedded in society and the DNA. And even though one or two practices emerged to try to recapture sacred sexuality, they too, in the most part, were impure.

It was no one's fault. This was how it all played out. Until the grids began to be deconstructed, it was too difficult for these higher frequencies and remembering to return to Earth. But now is the time. The remembering is returning. All of these dark parasitical webs are being unravelled.

It starts with your own healing; your own embodiment. Every single being on Earth, regardless of their gender or sexual orientation, has the power to re-embody the highest sacred magic. They have the power to restore divine union and sacred sexuality to Earth.

Over time, just as we shared is happening at the multiverse level, gender will be returned to its original divine forms, as will divine union and sacred sexuality. And, beyond that, all will come back to one. But it is a journey. One you are all taking together.

Gender as divine expression

As you know, regardless of gender, you hold the divine feminine and divine masculine within. These must be in harmony. Your divine feminine is wild and bold and creative. She will bring the inspiration and expansion to empower you to literally change the world. But she cannot do it alone. She needs the divine masculine to create a safe container through which she can birth her creations and greatest service. He will hold loving boundaries to ensure her energy is not drained. He will bring the grounding and structure to convert pure frequency and divine inspiration into action. It is through the divine union within of these two energies, that you are able to walk your highest path.

Before the interference programs that brought forth the distortion of the wounded masculine and wounded feminine, all was in balance and harmony. It was a sacred interplay. As within, so without. Yet, for the distorted masculine to rise and dominate through patriarchal rule, the divine feminine had to be suppressed. Without her energy to bring balance, the distorted masculine reigned.

This is why you now see so much confusion around gender. Each soul chooses its gender. It chooses the body into which it will incarnate. But, because the distortions are woven so deeply into the fabric of your societies and your ancestral DNA, some souls coming in through their chosen gender feel lost as to how they can express the highest vision they hold for their incarnation. Because your society places so much emphasis on the external, they may not feel supported to heal the wounded masculine and wounded feminine within. Instead, they look to external ways to change or reject their gender.

For example, this has been prominent in many corporate workplaces. The societal portrayal of women as weak and emotional has led many women to adopt the distorted masculine in order to get ahead. They may struggle with how to dress, believing that if they dress in a feminine way they will be categorised as either seductive or soft. So, they may lean towards a masculine form of attire, such as power suits and dark colours.

They feel pressure to work harder than their male colleagues in order to achieve promotion. So, they may become hard, cut-throat and overly focused on outcome. This denies the valuable contribution of feminine intuition, empathy and creativity. And, without a balance of energies in the workplace, the culture becomes overtly patriarchal. Competition snuffs out co-creation. The disproportionate view of productivity leaves no space for expansiveness and higher levels of inspiration or evolution. And many, male and female alike, end up feeling burnt out and unfulfilled.

For others, the experience of rejecting the distortions of the wounded feminine and wounded masculine may lead to rejecting their own gender completely. For others still, traumatic experiences of sexual abuse or assault can result in negative perceptions of gender.

To add another layer, it is about more than what a soul encounters or sees reflected in society. It is also about the trauma and distortions that are stored in their DNA; their ancestral lines.

Many are struggling with the illusions and programs that have been embedded through the shortening of the human DNA. As you are aware, these distortions are built into the very foundations of your societies.

There is no doubt that unfairness, oppression, corruption and depravity exist in the societal structures. This was a result of the interference with Earth from parasitical beings. Yet, it can also be the case that what one sees and experiences in the external is a reflection of their inner turmoil. To journey back to wholeness, one must heal their divine feminine and divine masculine, and bring them into divine union within. This means healing their personal and ancestral trauma and returning to love and acceptance within themselves.

When you embody the Rainbow Frequency and come into wholeness within, everything around you shifts to match that frequency. Everything comes into service of your highest path. In this way, you create your reality. Your inner state of separation or wholeness shapes your outer experience.

It stands to reason that those who see inequality and unfairness everywhere are holding that frequency within. For they are plugging into that external reality through their own victim state. We are not saying that inequality does not exist. We just want to remind you that you are empowered to create your reality, and from this space you can more effortlessly bring about change. This means that, even those who are challenging the old structures of inequality, must do the inner work of unplugging from the wounded feminine (victim state) and come into wholeness within themselves.

There will be a point in the collective journey back to wholeness where rejection of gender will no longer occur. As each heals their own wounded feminine and wounded masculine, they re-embody the divine forms within. This ripples out. With time, Earth will come back to the pure expression of gender. The divine feminine and divine masculine are but two parts of the whole. It was always the highest vision that souls would be able to go

95

to Earth and choose to experience the genders, finding wholeness within. If that were enough for them, they could weave their highest service without the partnership of another. Or, if they desired the experience of divine union with another, they could choose this. Then they would come into an external interplay of the divine forms.

Knowing that, in the 'future', all confusion and rejection of gender will be healed does not diminish the value and efforts of those struggling with gender now. Yes, over time, all will be healed. But the inner work and embodiment of each person on Earth at this time, will pave the way. As long as one is acting from their divine love essence, truth and purity, they are walking a path of service.

Before all, there are two paths – that of perpetuating the disempowering parasitical programs, or that of healing and returning to divine union and sacred sexuality. Everyone, of any gender or sexual orientation, is empowered to embody this divine expression. They can fall into the old patterns of abuser/ abused, unfaithful/betrayed, user/used and so on. Or they can step into a higher connection of love, respect, truth, conscious co-creation and more.

Whether a person identifies as male, female, transgender, heterosexual, homosexual or any other expression, coming into divine union within and with another is available to them. As we have shared, divine union with another is the frequency and nature of the connection two people share. It is the act of loving and lifting each other, and embarking on the journey together as two embodiments of The All – the divine love essence.

Divine union and sacred sexuality are every single person's birthright. The distortions and parasitical programs are being broken from the inside, by each person making a choice to reject the disempowerment and reclaim their sovereignty and greatest magic.

The journey back to these divine forms is about remembering. A soul's deepest yearning will always be to return to their divine love essence – their Rainbow Frequency. If a soul encounters what they feel as overwhelming amounts of the wounded feminine or wounded masculine in their ancestral lines, home life or culture, they may feel a desperate need for love, acceptance, peace and a sense of safety. At the root of all this confusion around gender is a rejection of the distortions – of what is not in alignment with divine love.

Eventually, as all of the cosmos comes back to one, there will be no gender. There will only be wholeness. This is how we are, the Rainbow Race – your Unified Selves. However, at this point in the cosmic journey, the human experience includes gender. And it is through each person's healing of the divine feminine and divine masculine within themselves and their ancestral lines, that the purity will be restored to these embodiments. It will ripple out.

When it does, the old distortions will crumble. Women will no longer be made to feel inferior or shameful, or forced to adopt the toxic masculine in order to survive. Men will no longer feel driven by power and a desire to control, or feel shamed for being in touch with their emotions and expression of their own divine feminine.

As the divine feminine and divine masculine are brought into harmony within each person, the two will also be brought back to their divine forms within society.

Freeing yourself from identity traps

An ever-growing trend on your planet as more and more struggle with feelings of disconnection, is the attachment to labels. Feeling like one belongs to a group or community often eases a sense of anxiety and isolation. Coming together in purity and heart-centred connection is a wonderful thing. But this is not what takes place when one creates labels and attaches this to their identity. Rather, this process creates separation and highlights difference. It is an expression of ego.

These labels are playing out in many areas, creating ongoing ways to divide, differentiate and judge others. There is only one race of humans – the human race.

Yet, humans have divided and labelled themselves by race and religion. This was established long ago. Dividing humans and pitting them against each other was part of the disempowering programs. It was the source of wars, slavery and attempts to dominate.

These divisions continue to permeate your societies. There are the lists of characteristics or assumptions placed on each race. Purely based on their ethnicity, people are labelled as lazy, greedy, privileged, opportunistic, criminals, extremists and so on. And too often these quick assumptions or projections replace getting to know an individual.

In your current world, tradition and diversity can be wonderful things to celebrate. They can be embraced to discover the beautiful parallels and similarities. They can be explored to uncover different pieces of remembering. And, ultimately, these labels can be deconstructed to see that, underneath the illusions of separation, all are souls incarnated to have an experience. All are trying to remember their divine essence. All have similar desires – to love and be loved. And, essentially, each is on the journey to remember that they *are* love. They are the Rainbow Frequency. This deconstruction of the facades of 'difference' brings you back to the recognition that you are all one. All is love and love is all.

So, when we apply this to the topic at hand, we can see that there is also only one category of sexual identity – human.

We understand that the trend on your planet is going the other way. That sexual 'identity' is moving further and further into division. But we wish to invite you to unplug from these identity traps and come back to your truth. You are human. More than that, you are The All having an experience in human form. And you have the opportunity to reconnect with the greatest and purest magic there is – sacred sexuality.

Yes, when dating or meeting someone with whom there is a potential spark, the sexual orientation of each party is relevant. But in day-to-day life, a person's sexual orientation is just one aspect of who they are. It is part of a much broader and richer whole. Just as race does not define a person, neither does sexual orientation. People from different races have so much to share with each other – because it is about the individual and not the label. The same is true for those of different sexual orientations.

We share this because many are becoming trapped in sexual identity. They remove themselves from others who are not from their same 'sexual community'. This could include religious approaches to sexuality, polyamory or free love, heterosexuality, homosexuality and so on.

Everything becomes about their sexual orientation, from clothes to music, interests, social circles and social venues. In this way, they lose themselves and their individuality in this sexual identity.

It is human nature to want to belong and be understood. And this desire manifests through sexuality because it is coming from a place of longing to remember. Essentially, it is the desire to reconnect with The All, to remember the purity of the highest levels of sacred sexuality. Through the return to divine union and sacred sexuality, each rediscovers The All within and The All in every other. It is the ultimate belonging.

So, what we wish to share in this section is that you are all one. You are all having an experience in remembering and returning to your All-essence. We understand that there is comfort and expression in being surrounded by people like you. And this can be healthy and uplifting. Yet, when it becomes a box or label, it only serves division. It is often thought that being in a sub-community means being fully accepted for all that one is. However, ironically, it can breed conformity and loss of expression, because there are expectations of what it means to be part of that sub-community.

Yes, you can embrace your sexual orientation with joy. But do not let it own you or create a divide between yourself and others. Sexuality was never about division. It was about connection, sacredness and wholeness.

Each desires to be whole, to be love and to be one with all. This is the deepest yearning and driver of all. But another can never make you whole. Nor can a community or label. The wholeness must be restored within. It is about your own return to wholeness. When you remember that the divine – The All – was you all along, you free yourself from the great cosmic illusion of separation. And you can let go of labels and shine as the wonderful, whole being that you are.

Section 6

HEALING SEX DISTORTIONS AND TRAUMA

"Sweetheart, I finally got you a flight back to Australia. It's in six weeks when they open the airport in Lima. It took hours and many calls, but you have a ticket. Everything will be ok. I love you."

The sound of my dad's voice note brought tears to my eyes. I was so blessed. No matter where I was in the world or what I was going through, he was my rock. I dangled my legs under the rail and off the edge of the rooftop. The nausea was never-ending, but being in the fresh air and feeling the sun offered some solace.

"Was that your dad?" Raphael asked as he sat beside me. I nodded. "Well, that's good then. Right? That's what you wanted."

I extended my hand and he cupped it in both of his. We had broken up the day after the threat of miscarriage. But we had moved through it and talked about the bigger picture. Raphael was freshly out of a 10-year relationship. He needed to heal and rediscover who he really was. We realised that he wasn't ready for another relationship yet. And that was ok.

103

"You know I'll wait here until you've flown out. I'm not going anywhere until I know you're looked after." He kissed the back of my hand and offered me a banana. I shook my head and choked back the feeling of wanting to be sick.

A beautiful eagle flew overhead. My heart was grateful. For three years the animal messengers had been with me.

Raphael tapped on the railing. There was sadness in his eyes and I felt bad. He still wanted the baby. But the reality was that, even if he were an active father, I would end up doing it alone. If I couldn't work for a year, I would have to go back to Australia. Being there would trigger my chronic illness due to localised severe allergies. I had lived for 20 years in excruciating pain. There was no way I could raise a child that way.

Even without focusing on the practicalities, I could see the two timelines. The timeline of having the child felt like doom. It was dark and heavy, like depression and desperation. The one of not having the child felt light and expansive.

Yet, here we were, stuck in Peru with closed borders. For the first time in my life, I did not have sovereign rights over my body. As a Western woman, I never imagined I would find myself in such a devastating position. The thought of not having sovereignty over my body made me weep.

"Hey, hey," Raphael said as he put his arm around me and leaned his cheek on my head. "It's going to be ok. You have your ticket now."

He was right. I should have felt relieved. So why didn't I? Closing my eyes, I connected with that timeline. But I couldn't see it. I couldn't see myself boarding the plane here. Nor could I see myself changing flights in Santiago. And there was nothing when I tried to tap into arriving in Australia.

"Oh my God!" I gasped. "The flight isn't going to go ahead!"

"What do you mean?"

"I can't see it. That timeline doesn't exist! We have to find another way out!"

I was standing now and could feel the panic rising. Raphael tried to assure me that this was just stress and hormones talking. I stopped.

"Raphael, you know my abilities. You know how accurate they are. I am telling you – one hundred per cent – that flight is not going to go ahead."

The next four weeks passed by in a flurry of phone calls. Each hold time was longer than the last. Raphael tried so hard to get an exemption for me to fly on an EU repatriation flight as his partner. The airline said to call the Consulate. The Consulate told us to talk to the airline.

Raphael collapsed onto the couch. "I've tried everything. I don't know what is left."

"Ausangate. That's what's left. The only way we're going to get out of here is through sacred co-creation."

I called my Peruvian friend and made the arrangements. Two days later, Raphael, Auqui and I set off at 5am. The winding roads took us into higher and higher altitude. When we finally arrived at the tiny town at the base of the mountain, my goddaughter ran out to hug me. She took my hand and chatted all about school and the alpacas as she led us to the small and basic kitchen. Her father, my Shamanic Paqo friend was waiting to greet us. It had been too long since we had all seen each other. And I was acutely aware that if Ausangate wove his magic, which I was sure he would, this would be my last visit to the mountain for who knew how long.

After a quick drink of hot quinoa, we started the strenuous hike to my friend's land. I asked the mountain to go easy on me. He was known for using the physical difficulty of the climb and the unpredictable weather to break down people and bring to the surface what needed to be released. The pregnancy had already been so rough on me. Today, the hike was easy. And I silently thanked Ausangate over and over.

When we arrived, my Paqo friend waved me into the little mud brick room and laid out his mesa to read the coca leaves. This was always done before the despacho, the sacred offering. It was how they knew if the intention was supported and if anything needed to be cleared.

105

My stomach knotted and I felt a lump in my throat. This was a dear friend. But I felt ashamed to speak to him about this. Termination was not something they did in Peru. I worried that he would judge me or not understand. Sensing my fear and shame, he took my hand and looked deeply into my eyes. His eyes welled up.

"Hermana, todo va a estar bien." I nodded. Ausangate was my most amazing guide. He was the reason I was in Peru and had stepped onto my path. I knew my Paqo friend was right. Everything was going to be ok.

"Estás lista?" Again I nodded. I was ready.

After opening sacred space and honouring Pachamama, Great Spirit, the Apus and Mamá Coca, my friend threw the first leaves. He was in deep communion. Whispering and blowing into the leaves before each throw. I sat in full trust, sniffing through my tears.

After some time, my friend paused and looked at me. In Spanish he asked me, "Is he a good man?"

"Yes," I replied. He nodded.

"Why do you not want to have the baby?" There was no judgement in his voice. His eyes were full of compassion.

"Because I can feel it isn't the right path for me. I don't understand why this has happened."

He nodded and poked around at the leaves, delving deeper into their answers. He threw the leaves once more.

"You will not get back to Australia. The way is blocked."

I nodded. It was what I had already perceived. I breathed deeply as he threw the leaves again, praying that we would make it to England.

My friend pointed out the signs I knew to look for. The perfect edges with no breakage. The way the leaves had landed with the green side up. How the direction lined up to where Ausangate stood beyond the mud walls of this small room.

"You will get to England. Ausangate is going to open the way. There is a small obstacle," he said, pointing to a tiny partially-broken leaf that lay across the others. "Not to worry. We will clear this energy through the despacho."

I blew my nose noisily as the emotion overcame me. For two weeks I had been faced with closed borders and the impending doom of not being able to make a choice about my own body so I could follow my highest path. It was a huge relief to know we were getting our miracle.

"Is there anything else you want to ask?"

I nodded. In a squeaky and broken voice, I asked, "Is it ok? What I'm choosing? I don't want to be a bad person."

My shoulders shuddered as guilt and shame that I knew wasn't actually mine, washed over me. My friend paused and hugged me. He spoke softly in Quechua, words I didn't understand. But I felt the loving energy. When I was ready, he squeezed my hand and blew into the coca leaves.

"All is blessed. The baby is here with us," he said, pointing to a small and perfect leaf that was almost floating up to the side. "The baby is working with you. You won't understand it all until later. But you will get to England and all is blessed."

His words exonerated me, and all the women who had come before me. I cried for all of us. For the wisdom of the sacred co-creation of our wombs that had been stolen from us. For all the times we had been shamed and shunned for trying to live our truth. Something bigger was taking place today.

It was time to invite in the others so we could prepare the offering. Time seemed to stand still. Or perhaps it was moving and I was outside of it, looking in. I knew that through the depth of this pure magic and sacred ceremony, I was literally creating my reality.

An image flashed before me. It was something the grandfather medicine had shown me after the divine union and sacred sexuality codes had entered my womb. He had shown me here at Ausangate. I was a giant, towering over the huge peak of the mountain. My body was glowing and flowing with the Rainbow Frequency. Way down below, towards the bottom of Ausangate, was a grey mist, like heavy smog.

The grandfather had said, "You are above the control now. When you embody the Rainbow Frequency as you have, you will always be able to create your reality and weave miracles. Even their bureaucracy cannot touch you now."

As we moved outside, my Paqo friend handed me the despacho to hold and infuse with my intention. Finally, I understood. Something within me felt different. I was about to fly across the world when it 'wasn't possible'. I was here in sacred co-creation with the ancient wisdom keepers and the Apus. This was the true magic. This was what it meant to be a master creator.

My friend received the despacho from me and, with his final blessings and thanks to the Apus and Pachamama, he placed it into the fire. At that exact moment, a snowflake fell onto my hand. Then another. And another. I tipped my head to the sky and welcomed the flurry from above.

"Sia!" Auqui exclaimed. "You know what this means!"

I did. Snow and avalanches were the highest blessings the mountain offered. I could feel a deeper remembering emerging in my womb. There was no place for shame. The baby and I were making this choice together. It didn't make sense yet. But I trusted that one day it would. For now, I was acting from purity. And that's all I could do.

After some time, my Paqo friend poked around in the ashes with a stick. He looked to Auqui and me and nodded. The ashes were pure white. That meant the mountain had received our offering. Just then, the snow stopped.

Auqui smiled at Raphael and me. "You're going to get your flight now."

* * *

"When you return to the divinity of your Rainbow Frequency, you unlock the fullness of your creator force. You remember yourself as The All-essence and you liberate yourself from the illusions and false paradigms. You awaken and weave your greatest magic. But to step into this remembering, you must consciously unplug from all that has kept you from it."

Recognising sex distortions in culture

The indoctrination of the sex distortions begins early on. And it can happen so subtly that you are not even aware.

In more Eastern or religious cultures this may occur as sex being positioned as dirty and shameful. Children may be taught to be ashamed of their naked bodies. Societies may censor or block films, television shows or music with sexual content. Sex may be positioned as only for the purpose of pro-creation, or, in some cultures, only for the pleasure of men. At the most extreme, women may be mutilated to prevent sexual expression or pleasure. It may be witnessed and ever-present in society that any departure from the oppressions of this version of sexuality is punishable by imprisonment, physical harm, or even death. And anything outside of a heterosexual pairing, may be met with expulsion from the community or any of the fates above.

Growing up with this kind of oppression embedded so deeply into society gives little to no space for an awakening into sacred sexuality. The fear of ostracism or death is used to control and suppress. And it is witnessed from a very young age. In this way, you can see how deeply the webs of the parasitical distortions have ensnared cultural, societal and familial dynamics to keep people from reconnecting with their greatest magic.

Although suppression and shame around sex can also be present in more Western cultures, in the most part, the pendulum has swung the other way. Sex is reduced to parasitical expression. It is used to sell products and a way of life. In this way, sexuality has become a form of manipulation. It has been ripped from its spiritual and divine expression and, instead, associated with instant gratification.

In these cultures, it is almost impossible for children not to be indoctrinated. Perhaps it is through music lyrics and video clips, billboards, magazines, television advertisements, or more graphic content shared by an older sibling. As they grow into their early teens, many of the movies targeting their age bracket are about sexual rites of passage. This creates an expectation of becoming sexually active in order to be considered popular and not labelled as 'frigid' or a 'loser'. It puts pressure on girls to send naked photos to boys and have sex in order to be liked. And it makes boys feel they have to accumulate a list of early conquests to prove their masculinity and worth.

Teenagers may also be drawn into the darker energies of pornography culture. This portrays a parasitical and base expression of sexuality that young impressionable minds come to think is the norm. This version of sexual expression seems to be reflected everywhere they look – music, films and so on. So, the spark of divine remembering in their hearts is dimmed and ignored.

With so much distortion and illusion absorbed in the early years, it is easy to see how a person can become lost as they reach adulthood. Many simply surrender to the way it is done. They may even think there is something wrong with them that they feel, deep in their heart and soul, that this is not what sex was meant to be. Others may feel the desire to seek out something more real and aligned with the glimmer of remembering that they feel around sacred sexuality. Yet, because the true expression of sacred sexuality is all but non-existent, they may find themselves unintentionally celibate or, at the other end of the spectrum, caught in a false light program. And so it is that you have seen the rise of 'spiritual' communities around 'free sex', orgies, polyamory and open relationships.

We know it has been hard and confusing. You are surrounded everywhere by the parasitical distortions of sex that are designed to keep you away from your deepest cosmic connection. When you return to the divinity of your Rainbow Frequency, you unlock the fullness of your creator force. You remember yourself as The All-essence and you liberate yourself from the illusions and false paradigms. You awaken and weave your greatest magic. But to step into this remembering, you must consciously unplug from all that has kept you from it.

110

Liberating yourself from the distortions

When you acknowledge the different ways that the sex distortions and disempowering programs play out in society, you can make a conscious choice to unplug from them. This starts with being honest with yourself. Identify what you feel is a divine union expression from a place of love, integrity and sovereignty. Then notice where you are not currently in alignment with that.

Perhaps you have let friends, society or a previous partner make you believe that being in a committed relationship is 'boring' or 'unevolved'. Maybe past experiences of being betrayed have left you feeling that divine union and an uplifting relationship is not possible. Deep down you know the cosmic truth. You remember. And you must acknowledge the false narratives and trauma that you have adopted, so you can liberate yourself and come back to your true essence.

This first phase tends to be at more of a conceptual level. It involves feeling into your truth and redefining concepts of love and divine union, and the forms they take. Next, you can dive deeper into the behaviours and dynamics of being in a relationship.

If you are in a relationship, this could mean looking at how you show up for yourself within the relationship. Do you honour your authenticity and let yourself truly be seen? Or do you hide or modify parts of yourself, out of fear that you might be rejected or judged by your partner or even yourself? Do you have loving boundaries, so you can co-create with your partner but also take time for what your soul needs?

Then look at how you are showing up for your partner. Are you placing expectations or demands upon them? Are you looking to them to fill you up? Are you taking responsibility for your shadow aspects and steering clear of projections, manipulation and other expressions of the wounded forms?

If you are not in a relationship, it is still a similar process. Start with yourself. Remember that whatever you want from a relationship, you must first give to yourself. If you want to feel valued and loved, how can you value and love yourself more? If you want companionship and adventure, can you make more time for friends, meeting new people and creating your own adventures? Then reflect on past relationships from a place of witnessing them. Were there any ways in which you did not show up for yourself or your partner? Consider how you could do things differently by coming from a place of divine union within.

As we have shared, it all starts with divine union within. Your Rainbow Frequency is your wholeness – your return to the All-essence within. Anything you do to strengthen and harmonise your divine feminine and divine masculine within, will unplug you from the disempowering programs. And a key part of coming into the divine forms is to acknowledge where and how the distortions are playing out for you.

This is bigger than you may think. It includes all that you bring into your energy field. As you start to unplug, you will notice where external inputs no longer align or feel good. For example, songs or movies that glorify deception or base forms of sex, the low-vibrational effects of alcohol and recreational drugs, or being around people who treat their partners poorly. And you may find that you need to make positive changes to surround yourself with higher-frequency and more loving energies.

With so much shifting, it can feel a little overwhelming. One of the biggest blocks many face is the fear of being an outcast. They feel that if they start to change themselves or share their new perspectives, their friends, family and/or partner will no longer understand them. And they worry about being rejected and isolated.

Firstly, if no one has the courage to awaken and return to truth, nothing will ever change. Secondly, as more and more do step forward, it makes it easier for others to follow. This creates a ripple effect. One's own embodiment of truth, sovereignty and divine love becomes an inspiration to others. It awakens a remembering within them. And they too start to feel the call to be brave and step out of the illusions and into their true alignment.

But, yes, it takes a greater degree of courage for those leading the way; those who will unlock and anchor the higher frequencies and the foundations of Rainbow Earth.

We understand there are nuances for those in relationships. We will address that further on. But let us start by sharing more broadly about this journey of transitioning out of the illusions (separation) and into cosmic truth (wholeness). It is not uncommon to experience a period of change where that which is no longer aligned drops away. This could be old habits, limiting beliefs and even people. Always when higher frequencies come in, they will push out that which is no longer aligned. This creates space for the new. And it allows your frequency to shift in order to attract that which is for your highest good.

There can sometimes be a period where it seems as though you are stuck between two worlds. This can feel a little lonely or uncertain. But know that this is a momentary thing. The new soul family, empowering habits, and whatever else you have created space for, are on their way. Think of it as a deeper layer of ego death where you are called to let go of control and the comfort zone. And see it as an invitation into deeper trust of the universe and your power as a master creator.

Use the in-between period as time to come into deeper expansion. This could be something like taking a spiritual course or signing up with a mentor. Or it could be expansion through committing to a personal project or learning a new skill. Whatever you choose, make sure that it is facilitating your greater connection with yourself. It is not about looking to another for validation. Rather, it is a beautiful co-creation with another or others who shares their gifts in a way that inspires and empowers you to come into greater expression.

Also make personal time to connect with your star family and guides. Do not get fixated on what form that takes. Perhaps you will see and hear them. Maybe you will channel by voice or writing. Or it could be a sense of connection without anything tangible. There is no right or wrong. It is about deepening connection and remembering that you are not alone. The more deeply you align to your true frequency – your divine love essence, the more easily new friends, community and answers will flow towards you.

Healing shame and trauma

We wish to assist you now with removing shame around sexuality and sexual trauma. We know that the pathway to remembering your sacred sexuality can be challenging. As you start to remember, the healing process will begin. Yet, it seems to be a common part of the human experience that, in facing what needs to heal, one may be met with feelings of shame. There can be so many triggers for this feeling. Perhaps a person was sexually abused. Or maybe a person acted in sexual ways that they now see were not in alignment with who they truly are.

First and foremost, we want you to know that there is nothing of which you need to feel ashamed. Healing is a journey of remembering and growing. No doubt, you can look back at many aspects of your life from your current more enlightened space and see that you would have made different choices had you known the things you do now. Everything is experience. And your experiences are helping you to arrive at remembering.

If you have treated yourself or others in less than honourable ways, there will be a process of forgiveness and healing that you need to undertake. These actions could have played out in many ways, such as being unfaithful to a partner or being with someone else's partner. It could be memories of engaging sexually when it did not feel right. Perhaps there were moments of being thoughtless or disrespectful about another's feelings. Maybe there were indulgences in fantasies that were not safe or positive. The list goes on.

Be gentle with yourself. You have come into a world that is so far from the frequency of your natural essence. Yet, part of the agreement in coming to Earth, is to forget. So, each is processing the feelings of density and misalignment in their own way. Whatever judgements you may have of your past behaviours, remember that you were trying to find your way 'home' – back to truth and your divine union within. Be compassionate. Acknowledge the behaviours that you now see were not positive and take them as opportunities to learn and grow. Then forgive that earlier version of yourself. Their lessons have delivered you to the more enlightened place in which you now find yourself.

Even those who have been on the receiving end of sexual coercion, abuse or attack, may struggle with feelings of shame. This can be confusing. In the rational sense, they often know it was not their fault. But perhaps they wonder if they did something to bring these acts upon themselves. Or maybe amidst the trauma, their bodies had a physical response and they do not know how to reconcile that. Or they could worry about anyone finding out that they had such a traumatic experience and the stigma of being a 'victim'.

In these more traumatic instances, beyond the shame, there could be reluctance to 'letting go' and healing. The ego might say that to forgive or heal is to condone the actions of the perpetrator. This is not so. As we have shared, forgiveness liberates you. When you hold onto grudges or anger about past experiences, you tie yourself to that lower frequency and that timeline. And you keep giving away your sovereignty to the one who did you harm.

Remember that you are not your experiences. And they cannot keep you prisoner unless you hold on and keep reliving them. We know this can be hard to hear when the trauma is raw. But when you choose to heal, you will discover the gifts in even the most painful experiences. Some have chosen specific trauma so they can heal for their ancestral lines and end the cycle. Others will discover great growth, awareness and transformation as they heal. Then there are those whose healing will become a catalyst for their life's work. You are an alchemist. When you heal, you turn the muck into a precious gem. That is how powerful you are.

Whatever your experiences have been, reflecting on your sexual journey can feel messy and confronting. However, we wish to reiterate that this is about healing and awakening. Meeting your shadow aspects and trauma is always difficult. The ego will fight against this, preferring to avoid and suppress that which it does not want to admit or acknowledge. Yet, healing trauma and unifying light and dark within are necessary parts of coming back to wholeness. It may trigger a deep process of acknowledgement, forgiveness and letting go. It can feel like being cracked open. But once you are through this, you are met with beautiful peace and expansion. It is a liberation – freeing yourself from your 'demons', as the expression goes.

When you unify light and dark within, you are able to love yourself fully. There is no judgement or fear or self-loathing. There is no shame. Rather, there is compassion, acceptance and love. When you love yourself, you are able to truly love others. And you can make your way into divine union and sacred sexuality.

Interlude

Before we get into the practical guidance, let us pause to lift the energy by celebrating the joyful aspects of healing. We have asked the Channel to share a story below of something that occurred as she finished channelling this manuscript.

* * *

The silence was so deafening that it made my ears tingle. It was just past midnight on a Sunday night in London. Even in this quieter area, the noise was non-stop from sunrise to well into the night. But, right now, there was a stillness I had not experienced in London. The warmth of the cacao spread through my heart. As I closed my eyes, I felt that blissful feeling of being with the Rainbow Race. A moment later, I realised I was with them on their plane. We spent some time in this divine energy. No words. No exchange. Just being.

Then I asked, "Why was I called into ceremony tonight? Is there something I need to know?"

The landscape shifted and I found myself with the Egyptian and Sirius God, Ra-Horakhty. He had long been one of my guides. But two and a half months after my dad transitioned, Ra-Horakhty had stepped in and told me he was one of my galactic fathers.

It was comforting to see him before me now and I gave him a big hug. I had agreed to bring through the Rainbow Tablets Mystery School. The teachings so far had been incredible – beyond anything I could have imagined. And Ra-Horakhty was here on this quiet London evening to show me more.

"Come. We need to journey," he said.

He guided me and soon I entered the Rainbow stream of consciousness of my Rainbow Unified Self. It was the collective consciousness of all of my fragments and incarnations. The first to step forward was my counterpart and I was surprised to see him. He took my hands and smiled lovingly. It was a smile I had only seen on the Earth plane in the fleeting moments when he had been in connection with himself through ceremony. Tears sprung to my eyes. My counterpart wrapped his arms around me and kissed my head.

"Don't feel sad," I heard Ra-Horakhty say from behind me. "This is not about showing you what you cannot have on Earth. This is about showing you what already is, and always has been."

As I breathed into the moment, I finally understood. I had known all along that I could work with my counterpart on the higher planes. But the longing and loss of being on Earth without him had always been too much. Yet, over the previous year, I had consciously worked at healing the deeper layers of anger and resentment I had towards him. It had seemed that every time I thought I was finally done, a few months later another ugly layer would rear its head. Finally, I had made it all the way through. It was two and a half years since I had had to walk away from him. But the last remnants of the aftermath had been cleared.

I looked into the eyes of this higher version of my counterpart. He smiled at me knowingly. Now the energetic pathways were clear. We were finally free to work together on the higher planes, even though we had taken different timelines on Earth.

When we had been together as a couple on this physical plane, it had awakened the codes within me for the Rainbow Tablets to flow through. I wondered what would be next now that we had reached a much higher and more pure level of co-creation.

My counterpart raised his eyebrows and smiled. "We're only getting started."

Practical guidance for healing

Let us return to the process of healing your sexuality. We wish now to share some practical guidance with you.

1. Seek professional help where needed

Let us start by acknowledging that in some cases it may be necessary to seek more conventional help, such as counselling. If you have harmed another, have thoughts of harming another, or have thoughts of harming yourself, we encourage you to seek professional help immediately.

As a broader note, being on the path of awakening does not mean you have to turn your back on all things conventional. The shift to Rainbow Earth does not mean that all conventional professions cease to exist. Each on Earth has the opportunity to walk their highest path and be in their highest service. That encompasses a full breadth of old and new vocations.

If you need more conventional assistance, it does not mean that you are reducing yourself to a lower reality. We wish to clarify this as there can be a misconception that to be spiritually 'awakened', you must only seek help from alternative avenues. In truth, support can be brought to you through whatever means are best for your highest good.

2. Set up a support system

When you are embarking on healing, it is important to have a support system. Where the 'work' is not quite so intense, your support system might just be a trusted group of friends with whom you can chat, have fun and feel a connection to the possibilities that lie beyond the moment in which you find yourself.

Where the work is deep and a longer process, you might still need the above. But you could also benefit from more structured support through a safe container, such as a mentor or counsellor.

There are some key characteristics to look for in a support person or group.

118

Ideally, you want someone who:

- is trustworthy and will keep your confidence.

- is authentic, compassionate and carries empathy.

- has a good sense of humour – not to diminish what you feel, but rather to help you keep perspective and laugh at how crazy it is to be on Earth during the Great Awakening.

- holds strong and loving boundaries (we will elaborate on this).

You may have some close friends who fit this description. Let them know what you are embarking on in your healing journey and ask if they would be willing to hold space for you. Be clear about what this means to you. For example, you might want someone to know what you are working through in case you need to reach out. But perhaps you also want your privacy and do not wish to feel as though someone is constantly checking on you. Communicate your wishes so they know how to best support you. It is not about offloading emotional baggage onto another or pulling them into your process. Rather, it is about knowing that someone is there if you find yourself in a moment of needing to be witnessed, hugged or even have some fun.

Where it is deeper trauma or healing, this may be too much to ask of friends. In this case, it would be better to engage a professional. This could be conventional or spiritual. Either way, be sure it is someone with whom you feel safe in the way they hold space. Boundaries are an important aspect of deeper healing work. It lets you know how you will be supported and what to expect. And it prevents the space holder from enabling unhealthy behaviour, such as victimhood, dependency, aggression and so on.

Allow us to use the Channel as an example. She works with clients one-on-one through a personalised mentorship program. From the start, they know they are fully supported. But they are also given parameters of the Channel's role as a space holder and facilitator. This is to ensure mentees are empowered throughout the process rather than developing a sense of dependency. She does the same with her group mentorships, to ensure everyone is safe, respected and empowered in their boundaries. If any lines were to be crossed, the Channel would lovingly reiterate the boundaries and guide the participant back to the purpose and role of the mentorship.

We share this because not all support workers have embodied this. And it can mean that they are unable to hold safe space for the healing journey. So, it is important to consider these aspects when seeking a support person and/or group.

And, it goes without saying, that if a support person of any capacity makes sexual advances towards you, suggests that engaging with them in a sexual way is part of your healing, or makes you feel uncomfortable, then that is not in integrity and it is not for your highest good. In this case, please terminate the arrangement immediately. Even though this would be discouraging, it does not mean you are a bad judge of character or that you have failed. Sadly, there are those who take advantage of others. It is not a reflection of you and it is important that you do not take it on. Rather, it is an expression of their own unhealed separation within. When one encounters such a situation, we recommend that they 'cut their losses', re-align themselves and find more loving support.

If you are a participant in a group, be sure to hold your boundaries with others in the group. For example, if someone tries to form a connection with you outside of the group, connect with your inner guidance to see if this is for your highest good. If you feel it is not, you can politely decline. Expressing that you wish to keep healthy boundaries around your healing support is a valid reason that can smooth over any social awkwardness. If you feel the connection is for your highest good, you can choose to proceed. But be sure that the friendship does not centre around the trauma experience. If it does, it will keep tying both of you to that old trauma.

Now that we have shared the considerations, let us bring it back to the positives. Having a support network is an empowering and joyful thing. It means you are not alone. The beauty of sharing the journey in a healthy way brings wonderful gifts for all who take part. Afterall, you came to Earth to help each other remember. And co-creation is a key part of how you do this.

3. Lean into the process

As you know, the ego resists pain. When you move into healing and releasing, it is usually a painful experience. However, this is short-term pain and part of the catharsis – the process of transmutation. When you learn not to fear this process but rather embrace it, it becomes very empowering. You realise that no experience or emotion has the power to keep you captive. Yet, this is the downfall of the ego. In trying to 'protect' you from the pain, it keeps you in an unhealed state. The pain is perpetuated, with no end. And that is far worse. So, if left to run the show, your ego actually becomes your captor.

We share this so you can recognise the impulse to resist or suppress what needs to be healed for what it is. It is a misguided attempt by the ego to protect you. In reality, it condemns you to ongoing suffering and keeps you from reaching your greatest joy and highest expression. This increases feelings of despair about not achieving what you came to Earth to do, and not being who you truly are.

Seeing through this illusion empowers you to choose a different path – the path to sovereignty and wholeness. It empowers you to step forward into the 'fire'. Because that is what it can feel like. Yet, it is a fire of initiation. A fire of growth. A fire of transmutation. When you lean into the process of healing, you move through the trauma and pain, and you liberate yourself. You bring the shadow back to love. You come into greater wholeness within. And you step into the expansion and magic that has been awaiting you.

Depending on what you are healing, this process may be easy or more intense. But do not give up. Even if you feel like you are being cracked open. This is the shedding of the programs, the hurt and everything that is not you. The sense of being cracked open is allowing more of your true essence to emerge.

The Channel has allowed us to reference a part of her process. Due to the trauma she encountered growing up, the Channel had a deep distrust and fear of the feminine. She had experienced the feminine as cruel, jealous, unfair and vindictive. So, she sought refuge in the masculine. Yet, because she was coming from an unhealed place, it was not the divine masculine. Instead, she adopted the toxic masculine. She placed blocks around her heart because she felt that if she did not let anyone in, they could not hurt her. And she became a workaholic, using productivity and accomplishments as a way to distract her from what she did not wish to feel or acknowledge.

When the Channel answered the call to Peru, she had to break down this program and reconnect with the divine forms. This was extremely confronting. Being in the feminine felt unsafe and there was much suppressed emotion to be released. Although it was a deep process, the Channel has now found deep healing, remembering and empowerment in embodying the divine forms. Previously, people described her as cold, hard and 'a robot'. Now they feel her as warm and authentic. This is her true self; the other was not. But it was necessary to lean into the healing and allow herself to be cracked open in order to rediscover her true self.

Even though the healing process can feel like a lot, there is no need to fall into victimhood or dramatics. Allow yourself to be a witness. Acknowledge the feelings and let them pass through. But do not re-attach or re-engage as a participant. If you need, ask your guides and team to bring forward the means to help you move through this and heal it fully. And know that often things are healed in layers. If something you thought you had already healed emerges, it does not mean that you failed. Nor does it mean you will never be free from it. You are simply being shown that you are ready to release a deeper layer of that experience or program. Always, on the other side, there are gifts of awakening, expansion and magic.

4. Foster the expansion

The healing process can happen in layers over time. Be sure to continue to grow and expand and live your life to the fullest. Everything does not need to be about healing. Some get stuck in the shadow work and never progress. This may be because they are expecting everything to be fully cleared before they move past it. Or they use it as an excuse not to step into their greatness. They keep looking for things to heal or looping back into the process, because if they never come out of it, they never have to embrace their divinity. The ego is very crafty at finding ways to keep you small.

Healing is not about stunting yourself or making that your entire experience. Continue to feed your soul. Listen to inspiring podcasts and read books that open your heart. Attend gatherings that feel joyful, such as ecstatic movement or an expansive workshop. Take time in nature and sacred sites. And have fun with your family and friends. Life is a grand experience. Your healing journey is just one aspect. Do not deny the rest of it.

What is more, your healing is not something you need to do alone. There are so many tools and practices to draw on. If you ask your team to show you what you need for your highest good, the answer will present itself. This could be through breathwork, plant medicines, counselling, an online course or a mentorship. The possibilities are limitless. And they may not be about 'healing'. Perhaps what you need for your highest good is rejuvenation and nurturing, such as a holiday. Or maybe you would benefit most from fresh energy, like learning a new language or starting a new sport. Be open to what calls you, without expectation. The path to awakening is surprisingly magical and can exceed all you imagine, if you just allow.

5. Let it flow with ease and grace

Although we have acknowledged that healing and breaking free from the old programs can involve initiations, we want to highlight an important distinction. This does not mean that healing and/or awakening needs to be 'hard'. This stems back to another disempowering program – that one needs to suffer in order to attain enlightenment. This is not the case.

It is true that challenging situations can be a catalyst. But this is often a way of shaking up things. It knocks you out of your comfort zone or state of being 'asleep'. Yet, that does not mean that everything needs to be hard or that you will only achieve breakthroughs if there is pain.

The more you listen to your heart and intuition, and follow it, the easier and more magical the journey becomes. There is a saying, "If the universe is trying to get your attention, first it will send a feather. If you ignore it, it will send you a brick. Then it will send a bus. Do not wait for the bus."

As you become more in tune and consciously co-create with the universe and divine flow, you find that all you need is the 'feather'. What we mean by this is that you do not need the proof or hard lesson to justify following your higher guidance. You simply respond, because you live in trust and deep connection.

The metaphor of the feather, brick and bus, shows you that it does not need to be hard. You make it hard by ignoring or resisting the universe's guidance and your soul's calling. The universe will always support your highest path. If you ignore this or keep choosing a lower reality, the universe will go to greater lengths to get your attention and affect change. The more you trust and let go of the egoic traits of control and resistance, the more your journey will flow with ease and grace. In other words, take the feather!

6. Be authentic with yourself and partner

It can sometimes be a strange thing to go through your awakening and journey back to wholeness while in a relationship. When two come together at a certain point in their paths, there can be a perception of who each person is. Yet, no relationship is intended to be frozen in time. This would make it stagnant.

Everything is impermanent. Everything is in a state of movement. People are no exception. It is unrealistic to expect a partner to always be the same person. In fact, this would be unhealthy. A person who wanted the best for their partner would want to see them grow and flourish.

In many cases, this is so. There are those who feel free to share with their partners as they awaken into more of their gifts and remembering. Perhaps their partners respond in a supportive way. They might feel intrigued and join in. Or they might not understand it, but they accept and love all of their partner, even the more 'eccentric' aspects.

However, there are also those who feel fearful about letting their partners in on their journeys. Perhaps they do not want to be seen as having baggage, so they hide that they are working through some things. Or it could be because they have seen that their partner is dismissive or closed to anything of a spiritual nature. Maybe they worry that as their consciousness expands, their partner will find them 'strange' and no longer love them. Whatever the reason, it can lead one to deny or hide who they are.

This may work for a short period. But, eventually, it will feel too misaligned. It is not possible to come back to wholeness while simultaneously pretending to be someone you are not. You cannot be in your highest expression while hiding your expansion. To return to your true essence and walk Earth as the 'God' All-essence that you are, you must act in integrity. And integrity requires authenticity. This is how you shine at your brightest and share the divinity of all that you are.

There are two main areas in which people tend to hide their authentic selves from their partners. We should note that we are talking about 'standard' relationships here and not ones based on abuse or danger. The two instances are – periods of healing and periods of expansion.

We will start with healing. As we have shared, healing can feel messy. You might be faced with old pain or insecurities that you do not want your partner to see. Or it could be shadow aspects you have tried to suppress. A relationship where one or both feel they need to hide who they are or pretend to be 'perfect' is not sustainable. First and foremost, honour and love yourself enough to be authentic. Secondly, if you trust your partner, let them in on your journey. It is not about leaning on them or draining their energy. It is about letting them hold space for you in your vulnerability – allowing them to truly see you. This is the real meaning of intimacy.

If you do not trust your partner or feel safe being vulnerable with them, you must look deeper into that. Is the distrust coming from the partner because of their behaviour or views? Or is it coming from you because of a sense of unworthiness or having been hurt in the past? This, you can heal. However, in general, the first option can only be healed by your partner. You can talk to them about how you feel. And you can make sure there are no blocks on your end. But you cannot do the work for them.

If one or both parties is not willing to grow in a way that would foster trust, safety and intimacy within the relationship, then the question must be asked as to whether or not the relationship serves the highest good of those involved.

The other time someone might hide their authenticity from their partner is during a period of expansion. Awakening into more of your truth and gifts is a wonderful thing. It is the reason you came to Earth. So why would one hide that? Perhaps the partner's framework and views are constrained by cultural beliefs. If one suddenly became aware of their cosmic nature but their partner's beliefs saw this as 'evil' or 'crazy', then they might feel unsafe sharing their expansion. On a less extreme level, maybe one knows that their partner is just not interested in these things. Maybe they are passionate about politics or history or sport, but they have no space for the metaphysical, magical or cosmic.

In these cases, fears can arise around judgement and rejection. One might even consider stopping their path of expansion because they worry it will put too much space between them and their partner.

Here we bring it back to the movement of everything. That is the natural state of the universe. When something stops, it becomes stagnant.

Energy and consciousness are moving all the time. You are made of this. And movement is life. That is why you cannot hold onto that which makes you stagnant and holds you out of alignment with your truth. You came to Earth to remember. You came to awaken and shine. That is why your greatest promise must be to honouring yourself and walking your highest path. When you do that, it naturally benefits all, because it ripples out and creates the new Rainbow Earth.

What we are saying here, in a gentle way, is that if you cannot expand and flourish in a relationship, you must let it go. Because the alternative does not serve you. And it does not serve your partner. This still applies when there are children, because children need to see role models who are brave enough to live their truth and share their greatest gifts.

So, provided it is safe to do so, open up to your partner. Just as you have changed and grown, your partner could as well. Give them the chance to meet you. In divine union, two embark on their journeys together. They lift each other and hold space for each other's greatest expression. Your partner cannot do this if you do not let them in.

That said, it is also important to be in tune with your partner's needs and take them on the journey. If you have been awakening in secret for a year and suddenly have expansive cosmic awareness, it is not really fair to drop that on your partner all at once. There may be a process of introducing concepts in a more digestible way. You could also let your partner know that this is not about them having to believe the same things or come to the same workshops or events. It is more about you knowing that you are witnessed and loved unconditionally. It is about feeling free and supported to be your authentic self. And for your partner to know that you are not placing any expectations on them. They are also free to be their authentic self with you.

Yes, there are divine unions where both are on accelerated paths. However, there are also divine unions where the two are quite different. One might be very cosmic and pursuing work and creations in the new way. The other might be in a conventional profession. This does not mean the union cannot work. On the contrary, it can actually be a beautiful harmonisation of Earth and star energy. In this case it becomes more about core values and embodiments, such as being honest, kind and encouraging to each other. The partners' ways of interacting with the world might have different forms. But both are putting loving and uplifting energy into the world and into their relationship.

That said, we do wish to acknowledge that in some cultures it is not possible to be open about expansion or leave a relationship when it is not right. It is unlikely that those in these confinements would have access to this manuscript. But we do not wish to ignore it. Each soul chooses different experiences for their lifetime. There is not one clear answer here. Some will choose that the consequences for seeking their liberation are worth that moment of honouring their souls' calls, even if it costs them their lives. Others will choose to keep secretly embodying the remembering within, as best they can. Some may secretly work on clearing their ancestral lines. Others may surrender to the confinement and give up any thoughts of unification and wholeness. While it is sad for anyone to be faced with such difficult decisions, your world is evolving. It is breaking free of eons of energetic tampering and parasitical programs designed to keep humans feeling hopeless and fearful.

Each person who is able to choose love, unity and wholeness, does it for all on Earth. They do this for the ancestors before them and the generations to come. This wave of remembering ripples out and brings others into the remembering. And, over time, it destabilises and exposes the old constructs.

So, be brave. Be your authentic self. And honour your expansion.

Section 7

PREPARING FOR SACRED SEXUALITY

The unfamiliar room was flooded with the light of the full moon. It was 2am but I was wide awake. Even at this time, there were sounds of the big red double-decker buses driving past. It felt so strange to be in London. Yet, here I was, on day three of the mandatory self-isolation period.

It had been a wild experience to fly out of the military base in Lima. We had had to wear masks and face shields. I could barely breathe and the band around my head had given me a headache. On top of that, our only meal on such a long flight was a paper bag with a sandwich, cookie and kit kat. I was gluten intolerant. I was also almost nine weeks pregnant and had needed to eat. The last three hours of the flight had been spent going back and forth to the bathroom. But we made it. Against all odds, we had made it.

Just three days after the ceremony at Ausangate, we had received confirmation from the airline that I was granted an exemption to fly with Raphael. It had been an enormous relief after such uncertainty. Yet, the following day, they let us know that Spain would not permit me to transit. Raphael looked defeated. But I knew the power of Ausangate. And I remembered what Grandfather Wachuma had told me. "Even their bureaucracy cannot touch you now."

I had known I had the power to do this. So I had tapped into my multidimensional abilities and called in all of my team. I asked to be guided as to the right action for the highest outcome for my highest good and the highest good of all.

"We need to write another email," I had said to Raphael. "Let me do it. I know what to say."

The notification that Spain would allow us through came just 24 hours before we needed to fly to Lima. I packed my whole apartment in a 14-hour window. With only two bags of luggage, most had needed to be donated. It was brutal. Everything had to earn its place in my luggage. When it came to my 20 journals full of my deepest thoughts and channellings, I wept. Some were from years ago that I had deemed so precious that I had brought them from Australia. Others documented my journey with the Rainbow Race, Egypt, my twin flame and more. It had hurt to throw them out. But there was no other option. I had to trust that anything I needed to remember was stored within me. It was a powerful lesson in non-attachment.

My phone lit up and pulled me back from my thoughts. It took a moment to register again that I was in London. I picked up the phone and viewed the preview on my screen.

"We regret to inform you that your flight from Cusco to Sydney has been cancelled…"

I smiled and put the phone back on the nightstand. It was all as I had seen. The fact that I had made it here meant I was exactly where I was supposed to be.

Suddenly, I felt a loving energy above me. The air seemed to glow with an illuminated essence. I had already done my Rainbow Pyramid sacred design before bed, so I knew this was a benevolent energy.

A sensation in my womb and heart made me gasp. It was the spirit of the baby! Tears instantly started flowing down my cheeks and my heart expanded.

"You have done well," the being said. It was beyond gender and carried the frequency of an ascended master. "This was never about me incarnating. I have already completed my Earth walks. This was all to support you in walking your highest path."

I was confused. The last few months had been so gruelling.

"You had been asking for your new timeline to come in. You knew your time in Peru was done. Yet, with the border closures, there was no way for us to relocate you. Pregnancy was the only way we could open the pathway for you. Raphael agreed to be in service in this way."

My mind was spinning. Could this really all have been part of a higher divine weaving? I thought back to the moment in my old apartment when I had seen my new timeline land like a tornado touching down. Just minutes later Ausangate had instructed me to look on Airbnb for my new apartment. And

Raphael had been told to stay in Cusco rather than fly out with all the other tourists. Then there was the fact that he had met me on the multidimensional plane a year and a half before we met in real life. The older, or 'sick from pregnancy' version of myself had met him at the Temple of the Moon. And he had travelled to me on a Rainbow highway.

Again I gasped. Was this really possible?

"Yes, dearest one. You have agreed to be the vessel for important work and we are supporting your path. It is time to remember that the womb is a great cosmic portal. It is not only for bringing a soul into incarnation on Earth. There are many ways for the womb to enable co-creation between the realms."

The ascended master continued to share with me. The cosmic codes in my womb began to stir. It felt like shooting stars. I couldn't believe what I was being told. But I knew it would end up going in the book. All that I had experienced was a deeper level of embodiment. How could channelling this great cosmic remembering require so much?

"Is this why the ceremony to release you didn't work?"

I felt the spirit's loving affirmation. So many pieces of the journey were clicking into place. Before we had gone to Ausangate, Raphael and I had come into ceremony on sacred land near our home. We had honoured the spirit of the child and I had released it, drawing on my multidimensional abilities to bring about a natural miscarriage. When it hadn't worked, I felt confused. After some days, my confusion had turned to anger. Why was I being put through this? Why was this soul not respecting my sovereignty?

Now it was clear. If the natural miscarriage had worked, I would not have received the exemption to fly. And, since this was all about moving me onto my highest timeline, it had to unfold the way it had.

"What if I had got it wrong," I asked. "What if I had decided to have you?"

The beautiful being smiled. It wasn't in physical form, but a smile that I felt.

"We knew you would connect with yourself and see the right path. I trusted you."

"But that's such a huge risk," I continued. "Imagine if you had been forced to do another 80 years or so on Earth!"

I felt the ascended master gently laugh. "Dearest one, it would not have been so. For that was not my highest path. If you had gone ahead with the pregnancy, you would have experienced a still birth. While this experience is called in by the souls of some women, it was not needed by you. So, here we are. We know it has been hard and confusing. But we have arrived. All is blessed."

They were the words my Shamanic friend had used. I remembered that the mountain had told him that the baby was working with me and one day I would understand. Never in my wildest dreams could I have imagined that all of this had been a higher weaving to bring in my new highest timeline during such challenging times on Earth.

"Thank you," I whispered. My heart glowed as I felt the loving heart transmission from this beautiful master.

"Wait! Will you be with me? On the day... when I get it done?" The being gave me the comforting sense of affirmation. And then it was gone.

A week later, I rose just before sunrise. The rays splayed from behind the clouds like magical blessings from the higher realms. I had been through so much turmoil and emotion over the last few days. The hormones made me second guess myself, even though I knew this was the right path. Today was different. Everything felt lighter. Clearer.

I made cacao and came into ceremony. There was so much to honour, heal and release. And there was so much gratitude I needed to express. The divinity of higher weaving was beyond comprehension. When it was time, I gathered my flowers, drum, Florida Water and crystals for the offering, then ordered a ride.

A tall guardian tree summoned me when I arrived at the park down the road from the clinic. I asked permission to make my offering there. It was lovingly granted. Part of me felt sad that Raphael hadn't come. He had made it clear he would bring me anything I needed and be there for me over the coming days. But to come today was too much for him and I respected his journey. He hadn't experienced the messages from the 'child' personally. And on the human level, he still wanted to have the baby. I believed that one day, when he was ready and with the right person, he would receive his wish of being a father.

As I opened the sacred space, the spirit of the child joined me. Again, we had a loving and expansive exchange. Then it was time. I completed the Earth offering to send this beautiful spirit back to the higher realms with a safe and protected journey. Right then, a tiny robin landed on the edge of my offering. It looked at me intently, peacefully comfortable being so close to me. And I knew that, as it always had been, "All was blessed."

In the change room at the clinic, I called in my whole team. I didn't like the idea of being under anaesthetic. I made sure that they would be waiting there to receive me. After being led into the procedure room and talked through the process, I was injected with the anaesthetic. Within a few seconds, my eyes closed.

I found myself inside the great pyramid. My amazing Sirius star family were there – Isis, Thoth, Ra-Horakhty and more. So were the Lyran white lions. And I was aware that I was in my Lyran form. We were laughing and catching up. Then we began to discuss important things. Before long, a voice interrupted us. I looked to my side. A lady in a green cap and green shirt was calling my name. What was a scrub nurse doing in the great pyramid with us?

"That's it. Open your eyes. It's time to come back now. Everything went well. We're going to wheel you into the recovery room."

I tried to find my way back to the pyramid. What had we been talking about? I wanted to remember. But the moment was gone. I had to trust that, on some level, I did remember.

About 20 minutes later, I checked out and received the little bag with the medical symbol on it. It was important to me to do this the right way. The energetic spirit of the ascended master had been released. But I wanted to honour and bless the physical part of this co-creation too. I had already

135

planned a trip to sacred lands in a few days. My heart knew that the perfect magical forest would present itself so I could return this energy to the Great Mother.

As I arrived home, I knew that the following days would most likely deliver crippling pain. Once that settled, there would be more womb healing to do. Right now though, I felt peace. And excitement. Finally, I had arrived. The heaviness had lifted. The sacred weaving was complete. All that the ascended master had taught me would go into the book. It had revealed to me deeper layers to the embodiment of sacred sexuality and the womb as a portal. And when I was ready to start channelling the book again, it would be shared with the world.

* * *

"To prepare for sacred sexuality, you must open yourself. It is an act of opening yourself to the experience, the remembering and your partner. And it is an act of opening yourself to you. Allowing yourself to be truly seen by you. In doing so, you shake off the shackles of disempowerment and illusion and give yourself permission to experience the full power of sexuality in its greatest magic and sacredness."

Opening to sexual expression

As we have shared, there are so many narratives, opinions and judgements around sex that it can block your connection to your sacred sexuality. When you are preparing for sacred sexuality, the first step is starting to recognise these distortions and programs and consciously unplugging from them. We have covered this in the previous sections.

The next step is opening to your true sexual expression. This is beyond all the stories and pre-conceived ideas. It is about giving yourself permission – permission to be authentic and seen. Moving into sacred sexuality can feel vulnerable. It is a space free of egoic masks and 'performances'. You are not playing a part, being what you think your partner wants. You are not hiding behind props or additional people.

It is just you and your partner. In this most real state, you are allowing yourself to be seen as your God/All-essence. This is the most beautiful expression there is. Yet, it can feel confronting at the start. Why? Because one of the most disempowering programs implanted on Earth is fear of your greatness. This means you fear seeing yourself and being seen. At the deepest level, it is fear of the divine.

Many are comfortable with the idea of an external God or divine force, especially if this external deity has power over one's life. Frameworks of external beings who punish, judge or decide if you are worthy of being welcomed back to 'paradise' after this lifetime, operate within the program of disempowerment. Because it allows people to feel inferior. It makes them feel that they have to meet certain requirements in order to be loved and worthy.

So, the realisation that you *are* divine love is a huge departure from the narratives of control and disempowerment. It is the realisation that you *are* worthy. You *are* loved. And you *are* love itself.

It is the realisation that God/The All is not external. Rather, you are The All, as is every other being in existence.

This understanding brings an awareness of your greatness, your purity and your power as an expression of the divine. And while this is the most magical and wondrous remembering to uncover, it goes against all that you may have been led to believe.

This disempowering program is embedded so deeply into your societies and social conditioning, that most feel that they cannot be their authentic selves. They feel they need to be a certain way to be 'worthy'. They feel they need to play different roles as the husband/wife/partner, the boss/employee, the son/daughter/child, the friend of a circle that sees them in a certain way. And so it goes on.

Yet, when you move into sacred sexuality with your divine union partner, all of the masks are dropped. Divine union brings you into great intimacy – intimacy with yourself and your partner. The act of sacred sexuality is the act of allowing your most authentic self to be seen, witnessed, held and honoured by another, as you do for them. And these partners lay themselves bare to come together and co-create as creation itself.

You do not have to be completely whole or healed in order to move into divine union and sacred sexuality. We say this to remove the excuses of feeling too 'damaged' or not whole enough to move into this higher remembering.

Yes, all of the work you do on yourself to heal trauma, release limiting beliefs, unplug from the programs and come into wholeness will serve you well. But the true key to divine union is the willingness to show up. It is the promise to take responsibility for your behaviours, triggers and patterns and to actively heal and integrate your shadow self. It is the commitment to honour, love and lift your partner and knowing that, in order to do that, you must first commit to honouring, loving and lifting yourself.

So, it is a journey. And that can make being fully intimate and seen feel vulnerable at first, because you might be used to hiding parts of yourself. However, the act of this intimacy – of being completely real and raw and sovereign with another reconnects you to your All-essence. It allows you to see your beauty and purity and divinity beneath all of the perceived 'imperfections'. And it allows you to tap into that pure creator force energy and co-create with another 'God' force through the act of sacred sexuality.

In this way, to prepare for sacred sexuality, you must open yourself. It is an act of opening yourself to the experience, the remembering and your partner. And it is an act of opening yourself to you. Allowing yourself to be truly seen by you.

In doing so, you shake off the shackles of disempowerment and illusion and give yourself permission to experience the full power of sexuality in its greatest magic and sacredness.

Awakening through self-pleasure

Before we get into the beginning stages of accessing the highest levels of sacred sexuality, let us share about healing and awakening sexuality through self-pleasure. Many hold trauma or blocks around their sexuality. It is not uncommon for a person to try to overcome or ignore their sexual trauma by taking on sexual partners. While you do not have to be fully healed before you take on a sexual partner, the best place to start is with yourself.

The practice of sacred sexuality with another is a safe and loving container. It is explored through divine union between two sovereign beings who have chosen to walk alongside each other. There is a foundation of love, co-creation and honouring each other.

In order to feel safe opening up to this kind of co-creation in a union, it helps to already feel safe with yourself. This applies to all aspects of self, including feeling safe to face your shadow aspects or those parts of yourself that you may find ugly. But what we wish to focus on here is feeling safe with yourself sexually.

Many feel uncomfortable in their bodies. In part, this can be a starseed reaction to the more dense frequencies of human DNA. But there are also many other factors. Very few people feel completely comfortable naked. This might seem strange given that this is your natural form. But, from an early age you are taught to hide your bodies. In societies, the naked body is criminalised and often linked to sexual deviancy or predatory behaviour. What is more, you face societal pressures to be 'perfect' – to look a certain way. And this leaves many feeling ashamed, embarrassed or critical of their bodies.

For men, there is pressure to have the perfect penis. It is hard to find a man who is not insecure about his manhood. He may worry it is too long, too short, too wide, too thin, too curved, and so on.

For women, there are fears around the vagina. She may worry about the smell or that it is too loose, too tight, too wet or not wet enough. In most cultures, it is taboo to talk about these things. So, many women take on an idea that the vagina is disgusting or ugly.

Added to this is the pressure to perform sexually. Both parties may feel that they have to be acrobatic and inventive. They may fear that the other will find them boring or not 'experienced' enough. And, with the societal expectations around dating in the more Western countries, sex is expected very early on. Often, this is even before it is a relationship. So, rather than sex coming from a deep expression of spiritual connection, it is coming from a place of physical desire or even a sense of obligation and expectation. This places even more emphasis on the body and performance, which can bring insecurities to the surface. And often it does not feel safe.

So, how can self-pleasure help you to feel more safe and connected with your sexuality? Firstly, it is about getting to know your body. We are going to ask you to reframe what you think of as self-pleasure. It is not about a quick path to climax. It is also not about turning to a low-frequency stimulant, such as pornography, to arouse yourself.

This is about genuine connection with your body. When you are truly connected to your own body and feel safe within it, you are more free and present when you engage in sacred sexuality with another. You are able to show up for them more. Because, rather than focusing on yourself – how you look, how you perform and so on – you can focus on your partner. In this way, the two of you can come into a beautiful divine flow. Think of the infinity symbol. Energy cannot flow freely out and back if the energy is tied up and blocked.

As this kind of self-pleasure might be new to you, allow us to share some ways to connect with the body.

Get familiar with your body. You would be amazed how many people do not really know their bodies. Take time to look at yourself in the mirror. This is done without criticism. Ideally, it is done from a place of deep love and appreciation. This is the vessel that is carrying you throughout life. It is the facilitator of every experience you wish to have. If you do not feel you can love your body yet, bring yourself into a state of neutral witnessing. Notice the texture of the skin. The moles. The curves or muscles. The shapes. As you are a tactile being, you may even wish to use your hands as you take in your body.

Embrace being naked. If you are like many, it could be that the only time you are naked is in the shower. Create more time to be naked. This could be sleeping naked. Or playing music and dancing a little before you get dressed. Or you may want to swim naked in a safe setting. When you can accept yourself in your naked form, it releases the pressure of being naked with another. You may even feel to be naked with others in a non-sexual way. Perhaps this is through ceremony, swimming or sacred dance with a safe group of friends. The intention must be pure – it is not about sexualising others or being sexualised. This comfort with being naked and being seen naked helps to release pressure and fears around being naked with a partner. It allows you to be more at ease and accepting of your body.

Explore sensuality. You have many senses. In the 'sex industry', this has largely been used to manufacture and sell gimmicks that act as distractions to true sexual connection. Again, it becomes about performing and 'making things interesting'. Yet, true sexual connection is more powerful and 'interesting' than any could imagine. And there is a way to involve the senses to support sensuality and sacred sexuality, rather than stealing focus. We invite you to tap into the senses as a way of opening more deeply to the connection within and, eventually, with another. Perhaps there are certain smells you enjoy, such as incense or essential oils. There may be music that opens your heart and connects you with a sense of bliss. Dimmer lighting or candles may evoke a sense of the mystical and spiritual. As you deepen your connection with yourself through self-pleasure, you may wish to explore some of these ways to engage the senses to enhance and support the connection with your sexual creator force.

Move the energy in your body. As you have life experiences, energy can get stuck in your body. Exploring forms of movement can unlock pockets of stuck energy in the body and allow for greater flow of sexual energy. Men in particular tend to have tighter muscles, especially due to the forms of exercise and sports that they often favour. Taking part in yoga, breathwork, ecstatic dance, or even the Temazcal (sweat lodge) can be great ways to help the energy in your body to flow.

Clear the body of past experiences. Sexual interactions involve an exchange of energy. It is important to clear your bodies (physical, emotional, mental, energetic and spiritual) of past sexual experiences. This helps you to realign to your true frequency. And it creates space for your current or new partner. There are many ways to clear this energy, including the practices we just mentioned above. To find what is right for you, ask your body what it needs. You can also ask your team to assist you with bringing forth the right avenues. But always be discerning. Choose practices and offerings that feel in truth and alignment with you. And know that it is never required that you engage in or witness sexual acts in order to clear your sexual energy.

Bond with your sexual organs. Too often the experiences around connecting with one's sexual organs is all about physical gratification. When it comes to self-practice, it can be quite functional – all about obtaining climax. As you start to discover sex as the experience and expression of your divinity, you may need to rediscover your sexual organs. Be more loving and nurturing with them. Connect with their purity and power. They are the Rainbow Bridge to the All-essence. Your sexual organs are sacred vessels for great magic.

Women may want to adopt practices such as working with yoni eggs. Men may want to work with allowing the energy to flow beyond the penis. By this we mean combining stroking with longer strokes that take the energy up from the tops of the thighs and even up into the chest. By bringing some longer strokes or even spiralling motions, the sexual energy is encouraged to travel rather than culminate in the shaft of the penis.

And you can start to consciously engage your sexual organs without any touch or physical stimulation. This can be done through connecting with your Rainbow Frequency and wholeness. Working with conscious deep breathing right down into the pelvic and sexual area will stimulate the creator force sexual energy. You can come into this connection with your sexual organs and the cultivation of your creator force energy through certain ceremonies or energetic practices. Although, be mindful that many of the 'sexual' teachings currently on Earth are still holding distortions. So, we invite you to choose more 'neutral' practices in order to uncover the remembering within yourself.

Some examples are cacao ceremonies, other plant medicines, drumming and breathwork. Approach your intention to awaken your creator force energy from your purity of heart.

Explore orgasm as a state. We will share more deeply about how you can use fantasies positively, as these can be beneficial in self-practice. For now, let us skip ahead to the orgasm. Through your self-practice you can start to explore orgasm not as a moment or climax, but as a state. We know there are tools and toys to help people maintain a longer and ongoing sense of orgasm. We are not talking about that – for those are focused on the physical stimulation and are not 'orgasmic' in the true sense of the term. Here we are referring to orgasm as a state of oneness. It is the act of transcending separation and experiencing yourself as The All once more. It is the purest form of bliss, because it is your natural state.

Through your solo work, you can practice extending the orgasm so you can actually 'be' that frequency. We will share later how you can do this. To begin with, you might feel that you need to use 'fantasy' to initially build the energy. Then move your awareness or focus from the fantasy into the energy itself. All of your focus goes into the blissful pulsating creator force energy. It is almost like diving into a pool. And you maintain that energy through your breath. Feel that each breath is expanding that energy. By this point you may find you do not need any touch because you are connecting with orgasm as an energetic frequency. And you can stay in this space for as long as you wish. If you have ever worked with the plant teacher, Wachuma, you may have already experienced this state. Now it is about learning how to cultivate that for yourself and sustain it.

As you become more in tune with the frequency and state of orgasm, you will notice that it is amplified and sustained from the heart, not the sexual organs. We will elaborate further in the following sections.

The energetics of fantasies

As you may be aware, everything is energy. Every action has consequences. And every thought sends out waves. We share in the first manuscript that time is not tangible. Rather, it responds to your frequency. If you feel you will not have enough time and send out those thoughts, time responds to this frequency and speeds up. Whereas, if you believe that you have more than enough time to do everything and consciously slow down time, this will be your experience.

This is true for everything. The multiverse is consciousness. Everything in existence is The All, having an experience in separation. So, it stands to reason that if everything is the All-essence, then everything is a constant co-creation. It is all responding to frequency and intention. This is what it means to be the master creator of your own experience. When you embody the Rainbow Frequency, you do this from an awakened place of love, unity and cosmic truth. And, because you are creating from a frequency that perfectly matches the essence of The All, all that you desire flows with great ease.

So, what happens when a person is carrying a lower frequency? Do their thoughts create ripples and create their experience? The answer is, 'Yes.' We have shared before that you can choose and create your reality. This also applies to your sexual expression.

There are those who adopt fantasies to create a sense of arousal. This is, in essence, a form of manifesting. Imagine that one were to fantasise about a loving and nurturing partner with whom they could express the highest levels of sacred sexuality. This would draw that energy towards them and help them to unlock deeper remembering. It may even send out a beacon call to their divine union partner, bringing them together sooner.

Now let us explore the other side of that. If one were to engage in dark fantasies, such as rape or torture, what would happen? They would attract that energy to themselves. This could be in the form of low-frequency entities and beings that feed on pain. If one were to delve into these lower frequencies enough, they may attract an attack on the physical plane or a partner who treats them in these ways. Or they may even end up being the perpetrator of a dark act themselves.

There is often a belief that fantasies are harmless – no matter how dark or violent. This is not so. They always have an energetic repercussion on the one delving into these realms. For these are not just imaginings. When one fantasises about harming another, they are literally tapping into the collective energy of perpetrators and taking that frequency into their energetic and physical bodies. And when one fantasises about being a victim, they tap into the collective energy of those who have been harmed and take that into their energetic and physical bodies. The world is not just a three-dimensional construct. You are a multidimensional being and much exists in the 'invisible' realms. It is as real as a physical object that you can see and hold.

Sacred sexuality and divine connection never involves harm to yourself or another. Not by act or thought. Not against one's will or even with consent. Any expression of sexuality that relies on harm, violence, domination, pain and so on, is rooted in the parasitical programs.

We use these examples to illustrate the bigger picture. Returning to divine union and sacred sexuality is more than just the physical acts. It is also thoughts and frequency.

With this in mind, let us share how 'fantasy' can help facilitate your sacred sexual awakening. You are no doubt aware now that sex and your creator force is so much more than you have been led to believe. It is not just about a moment of pleasure or expression of love. It is one of the most powerful ways you create. This is above all old notions of magic as potions and spells. And it can never be corrupted or misused. Because working with your creator force is the pure magic. As we have shared, it can only be accessed by those who are pure of heart and pure of intention.

We cannot share the exact details of the highest levels of sacred sexuality, because it must be remembered through embodiment – through living into it. Yet, we can take you right to the doorstep, so to speak. We will share more in the coming section. But let us start with fantasy. Many use fantasy to gain arousal through self-pleasure. Often, this fantasy is of a sexual nature.

What if the 'fantasy' or, dare we say, visualisation, was of what you were calling into being? What if, instead of trying to achieve orgasm (a state of touching The All) through imaginings of sexual acts, you did so through connecting with the greatest desires of your heart and soul? When you do this, you will find that the arousal is much quicker and often more intense. This is because in connecting with the desires of your heart and soul, you are energising and awakening the creator force. The remembering of yourself as a master creator is awakening. And by engaging in 'fantasies' of what you wish to bring into being, you put things into motion.

Energy flows towards that upon which you focus. We shared that negative fantasies will attract negative energies and events. But 'fantasies' of what your heart desires, will attract that. It already exists in one form or another on a higher-dimensional plane. As you connect with it using your creator force and through vibrating at the frequency of The All (orgasm), you draw it to you and onto this plane.

Purity of intention

As with all forms of working with intention and manifesting from a place of purity, there are some important dynamics of which you must be aware.

1. Always respect others' free will

Every being on Earth is sovereign. They have free will. When you create from purity of intention, you respect this and know never to interfere with or try to manipulate another's free will.

2. Leave the outcome to the universe

Bring your intention to the essence of what you desire, without attaching that to a specific form or outcome.

3. The universe (and multiverse) is infinitely abundant

We reiterate this to remind you that when you are honouring the two dynamics above, you never need to worry that in calling in what you desire, another somehow misses out.

Allow us to illustrate what we mean here. Imagine that you were wishing to call in your divine union partner. If you were to do so by naming or visualising someone specific, you would not be honouring the above dynamics. Trying to call a specific person to be in union with you does not honour their free will. It also does not leave the outcome to the universe. What if the person you had in mind was not actually the highest divine union for you? And, because this does not respect one's free will, it could be trying to take something that is not intended for you. For example, this person might actually be the highest divine union for someone else.

So, how could you connect with an intention of calling in your highest divine union from a place of purity? Well, you would bring it back to what your heart and soul actually desire. Perhaps this is a lasting divine union where you both love, honour and lift each other. Maybe it is one where you make each other laugh, inspire each other and have connected and cosmic sacred sex.

In this example, you are not attaching your intention to a specific outcome – a specific person. Therefore, all three dynamics are respected and the universe has the spaciousness to bring you the highest possibility.

You might wonder then, how you can engage in a fantasy or visualisation about this person if you do not know what they look like. It could be that they are there in a more etheric form and you are connecting with the way they make you feel and the energy flowing between you. It could be that they do take a form, but it is not someone you know or have seen before. If that is the case, remember not to attach to an idea that the partner being brought to you must look like that. Or you might not have visuals at all, but rather just go with the feeling and energetics. Where this is the case, you will often be able to bring more focus back to the creator force energy moving through you.

Using the creator force to manifest

Now that you understand the power of the energetics around thought and imagination, you can use it to raise your vibration. As we have said, energy will flow to that upon which you focus. But it is more than that. Think of this energy as a figure of eight. Energy does not just flow to that upon which you focus. It also flows back. You become a magnet for it. For, as we have shared, the multiverse is in ever-flowing co-creation. Everything responds to your frequency and intention.

We have also shared that connecting with your sacred sexuality is the channelling of your creator force. Your All-essence. What happens when you bring the two together? You can manifest and create with great ease. The deeper and more cosmic levels of manifesting and sacred co-creation are extensive enough to fill an entire manuscript. But what we have shared here and in the following section, will already greatly elevate your ability to manifest. You will be able to cultivate divine flow, miracles and blessings. And, as magical and incredible as it will seem, this is only the beginning of what is possible.

Section 8

PRACTISING SACRED SEXUALITY

Waving goodbye to everyone on the Zoom call, I closed the space and flopped back in my chair. Wow! What a session. When my team had asked me to share a small group mentorship on sacred sexuality, I had no idea how potent and expansive it was going to be. Part of me couldn't believe that with everything going on in my life, I was still able to channel and facilitate at these levels.

It had been nine months since I arrived in England and made it my home. So much had happened during that time. My fit and healthy dad went in for a colonoscopy and ended up battling for his life. All because of surgeon error. It was gut-wrenching. He had been so desperate to see me. Yet, flight after flight that I booked got cancelled. So, I did the only thing I could. I came into ceremony and connected with the Ancestor Star Keepers at Uluru. I asked them to help open the pathway for me so I could see my dad. And I offered to do anything they asked that was for my highest good and the highest good of all.

It was like they had been waiting for me. For hours and hours I had embodied Sirius codes that they said needed to be held on Earth. The next morning I woke to an email from the Government saying that I had a flight.

It was pure magic. My second miracle flight across the world during closed borders. It gave me precious weeks laughing and playing cards with my dad in the hospital. Now I was in London again and back to daily video calls with my dad. He was at home awaiting his next surgery – a metal plate to replace the missing part of his skull after an oversight by a nurse had left him on the floor with a brain bleed. It broke my heart that the most beautiful person I knew was enduring so much.

The roar of a motorbike jarred me and I stretched my arms above my head. It was the perfect time to enjoy the English summer and pop out the back to my balcony. A squirrel ran along my rooftop. I wondered if it was the same one I had found in my bedroom the other day when I had left my window open. As an Australian, I was certain I would never get over the excitement of seeing their gorgeous little faces and bushy tails.

The sun felt delicious on my skin. I sat down and rested my feet on the ledge. How deep were we going to go with this embodiment and awakening of sacred sexuality? We had already healed some of the big wounds and distortions. We had also received incredible activations. And now we were diving into a new exploration of pleasure and sensuality.

I ran my fingers up my bare arms. There had been such long periods between the touch of another, even just a hug. Seven out of my last nine months had been spent in lockdown. Even though I had Raphael's company for almost three months of it, that still left a lot of isolation. And there was something I had been ignoring. It was coming to the surface to be loved and healed.

I placed my hand on my womb. My body felt so unfamiliar. Since the pregnancy and my dad's battle, I had put on so much weight. I knew I was using food as comfort. It had brought me pleasure in a period of my life where there was so much heaviness. Yet I also knew I wasn't honouring my body. My usual slender and athletic frame was bloated and dense. Before the lockdowns, I had been so active. You couldn't live on the side of an Andean mountain and not be. But I had never been someone to exercise alone at home. After a year of inactivity, my muscles were stiff and my body felt neglected.

Again, I swept my fingers up my arm, enjoying the sensation. A pair of green parrots squawked as they flew overhead. For a week now, I had been thinking about joining a gym. But the thing I was avoiding kept stopping me. I squeezed my hand gently over my womb. The scary sensation of the tearing feeling was still fresh in my mind. Shortly after the bleeding incident in Peru, I had gone for an internal ultrasound. It had revealed tearing of the placenta wall. The doctor had told me I needed to be very careful. Even though I had realised by then that I wasn't meant to have the baby, I still did not want to end up in the hospital. On a subconscious level, I had become afraid of my own body. And I had disconnected from it.

The leaves rustled as a squirrel jumped from one branch to another. It was met with another feisty fellow defending his turf. A short squabble ensued. It made me laugh to watch their little dynamics. The trees behind my apartment were like an enchanted little park. I stood up and extended my arms out wide, acknowledging the trees with gratitude. As I sent love to them, I felt their love come right back to me. It amazed me that in a city as big as London, there was still so much magic to be found.

My heart felt so full. My dad was stable and back at home. And after a break of many months, the channellings for the second book were flowing once more. Each was richer than the last. It was the 'knowing' I had felt deep within since I was just a teenager. Yet I never could have imagined it would be so powerful.

On top of that, I had released my first original medicine music song, with five more in the works. I turned my face to the sky, basking in the sun's touch. When I opened my eyes, I saw the flash of a lion. Ro'Kay. I smiled. Of course he had popped in just as I was thinking of the music. That was, after all, his creation. My counterpart's destiny had been to bring through powerful medicine music. I had seen the global success and joy that was laid out before him. He had an incredible voice and an unbelievable ability to pick up an instrument and master it within a few weeks. But my counterpart didn't step onto his path. Just days after I had embodied Ro'Kay, he had told me, "Now you will bring through the music."

153

It had seemed crazy. I had never thought I had a good voice. And when I tried to play instruments and sing at the same time, everything went haywire. It was like trying to pat my head and rub my tummy. Yet, not long after I had returned from Australia, I had started channelling medicine songs. Like magic, a music producer contacted me out of nowhere for an unrelated reason. But we decided to work together and the first song was birthed.

A second pair of parakeets flew over me, heading towards the park. Seeing them in union made me think fondly of my counterpart. Our last interaction had been awful. In fact, it wasn't even an interaction. It had been four months earlier when I was desperately trying to get to Australia to see my dad. I had been on the Government wait list for seven months without any contact. The travel agent told me the only chance was to buy a business or first class ticket. Planes were only allowed to carry 30 people. So they would fill up the expensive tickets then cancel the economy.

It would have cost between $10,000 and $20,000 Australian for a one-way ticket. That was insanity! But it was my dad. I had to do whatever it took. At the time I had contacted my counterpart to ask if he could pay back the thousands he still owed me. He hadn't replied. It wasn't surprising about the money. But the fact that he hadn't even messaged to say he hoped my dad pulled through made me furious. As far as I had been concerned, my twin flame was dead to me.

Yet, with the teachings about divine union and sacred sexuality flowing through me like liquid rainbows, I only felt unconditional love for him. And it made me want to reach out. Picking up my phone, I sent my counterpart the link to my song, 'Phoenix Rise'.

I went inside and changed into workout clothes. The fabric had to stretch so far that I could almost hear it groan. Today I was going to reconnect with my body and start moving through the remaining trauma from the pregnancy journey. As I was about to walk out the door, my phone beeped. It was from my counterpart.

154

"I opened up your book for the first time a week ago. Felt a lot of love for you last night as I finished it. It's no surprise to hear from you today, but I do have to laugh. We're always connected. Thank you, I love the song."

I bounced down the four flights of stairs with a smile in my heart. Everything was in harmony in my world. It was about time after so many big experiences.

Then as I stepped onto the street, a niggling feeling rose inside me. I unlocked my phone and re-read the message. On the surface it was beautiful. But the omission made old anger rise. Four months ago I had asked him to pay back the money he owed so I could visit my gravely ill father. Was he seriously just ignoring that? He knew how close I was to my dad. Yet, he hadn't asked how my dad was doing. He hadn't even said that he hoped I had made it home.

The more I reflected on it, the more the old resentment festered. I had done so much healing to release this anger. But there were still deeper layers. And I knew why. On some level I was still waiting for him to pay me back. His empty apologies had always been followed by more toxic behaviour. Paying me back wasn't just about the money. It was about demonstrating change. It was about acknowledging the way he had treated me and showing some integrity.

My temples started to throb. Of course. This kind of energy was bound to manifest as pain. Today was meant to be about honouring my body. Going down this rabbit warren was the opposite.

As I arrived at the gym, I paused to take some deep breaths and exhales. This wasn't about my twin flame. It was about me. I couldn't pin my ability to heal on an act of integrity from him. I was just keeping myself hostage. It was time to let go of the need for a genuine acknowledgement or apology.

As the Rainbow Race had shared, I could only access the higher levels of sacred sexuality if my heart was pure. This deeper release was about liberating myself. I had waited my whole adult life to remember and experience the fullness of sacred sexuality. And I was ready to create more space and purity for the highest magic to awaken.

* * *

155

"You must be pure of heart and intention to access this highest level of magic. This is because there is no 'dark side' to creating as the creator that you are. When you create from this space you are remembering yourself in wholeness. Your dark and light within have unified, and you are creating as the Rainbow Frequency – the essence of divine love. You are literally creating with love, from love and as love."

Building sexual energy to become orgasm

No doubt, you are used to your sexual energy stirring and building in the root and sacral chakras. For many, it never moves beyond this. The base physical program of sexuality concentrates the energy around the sexual organs and sexual gratification. By restricting the flow of the sexual (creator force) energy, it keeps you from remembering your All-essence and the greater magic.

But the heart is the portal. It is the gateway to all that is. And the penis and cervix come together like a lock and key to unlock the Rainbow Bridge to the great cosmic magic. We wish to reiterate that here we are talking of the original designs. You are still able to fully access sacred sexuality and your All-essence if you are in a same-sex divine union, or working through solo practice purely from divine union within.

So, let us further describe the pathway of the creator force energy. First, you consciously connect with this force within. You do this through the purity of your intention to engage in sacred sexuality as your All-essence, as well as recognising the All-essence in your partner if you are in joint practice. And you use your breath. You deepen the breath and allow it to really travel all the way down to the sexual organs. Then you feel it circulate around the pelvic bowl before looping up for the exhale.

This will awaken the creator force energy in the root chakra. In flow with yourself for solo practice, or your partner for joint practice, you then draw the energy up from the root chakra and into the sacral chakra. This awakens the cosmic portal, the Rainbow Bridge within. It is your pathway to all that is, to experience yourself and your partner as creation itself. This can bring great sensations – bliss, ecstasy, tears of joy and remembering. The first time you experience it, you may find you climax right away and cannot move further. That is ok. You are re-opening and rediscovering pathways that you have not accessed for a very long time. Patience and presence are key. Let the journey be surprising and joyful.

To bring the energy up from the root to the sacral, you work with the breath. You do not need to repeat your intention. The intention is simply embodied. All that is required is your full presence. You must be fully in the 'now' moment. This is not a place for the head. And you must be fully connected with the body. This is not a time to be self-conscious or resist the human embodiment.

To help the energy rise, you also bring in movement. When you engage with the creator force energy in this way, it is impossible not to move, because it pulses through your body. You will most likely notice a wave-like motion with the hips and pelvis as the energy pulses and makes its way into the sacral chakra. For men this will be matched with the rise of the penis. The energy is both rising internally up through the pelvis and rising within the shaft so the penis is more in physical alignment with where the cervix (the cosmic portal) would be. Again, if you are in a same-sex union, it is not about a literal penis or cervix, but the energetic memory within the body of unlocking the Rainbow Bridge.

None of this is forced. It happens as divine flow – as remembering, something you have embodied and practised many times before. You are not willing the energy to rise or forcing it. It is just happening as a result of the connection, presence, breath and pulsating movement.

If you are working with a partner, you can come together into full sexual expression at any time after the creator force has reached the sacral. You may find that, to begin with, it could be a little hard to move beyond that level once you come into full engagement. But, with time, you will find it easier to connect with this full sexual expression as both a physical and energetic act. In this way, you will be able to keep the energy moving without reaching climax.

Or you will be able to reach climax and stay in that state for as long as you desire.

So, let us continue. You will then draw the creator force energy up into the solar plexus. This can be a little harder for men to begin with because the blood rushing to the sexual organs can make their sensations pool in that area. But, like anything, it gets easier the more you do it. The flow of the creator force energy causes what can almost feel like an explosion of sovereignty. At this point, some may climax and not be able to go further, because this sense of divine sovereignty is such bliss. As you become more accustomed to this true cosmic sovereignty, it will make it easier to move beyond this state.

The intensity of the sovereign state can often magnify the need for movement. Perhaps it is with a spiralling or figure eight of the waist and lower ribs. Or it could be a pulsing movement of the two bodies together. Sound is often also amplified at this point. By consciously drawing the creator force energy into the solar plexus, you tap into your own inner central sun. The highest levels of sacred sexuality is the multidimensional experience of connecting with all of your other fragments in their purity. This is you at your most sovereign. It is like a beacon call to all of 'you' in the multiverse. But, as it is fuelled through the creator force entering your inner central sun, you do not pick up the doubt, weakness or shadow side of these other fragments. You only connect with the purity (wholeness) of their essence. This is why this level of sovereignty can feel far beyond anything you imagined.

Remember that, if you are working with a partner, you are guiding each other through. This is a co-creation of two 'God' beings on Earth. It may sound like an internal process. But in the way that your bodies pulsate and move together, and the eye contact, which is a soul gaze beyond all physical form, you are reflecting each other. So, you are lifting each other as you go and amplifying the experience for each other.

From here, the creator force energy rises into the heart. This is where some will instantly be blasted out into 'The Dimension' – the place of origin outside of time and space. It is the place where we, the Rainbow Race exist. When you experience this, it is such a sense of wholeness and pure bliss. It is beyond what you have known as orgasm in the past. And it is the moment of becoming orgasm. You become that state. You are whole and one with everything. It is complete euphoria because that is the feeling of The Dimension. If you are instantly catapulted into 'orgasm' once you reach the heart, you can use the breath and movement to sustain this state. Rather than collapsing in and coming down from that moment of 'touching The All', stay with it. On a physical level, you are using breath and movement to circulate the energy throughout your body. We will not prescribe how to do this. But one option is to bring it into an infinity symbol. The cross-over point is at the heart chakra, then it expands out and loops at the root chakra below and the crown chakra above. And when you have more experience, you can extend it so the infinity symbol loops at the cosmic portal at the top of your auric field, and again at the Earth star at the base of your auric field.

If you are working with a partner, we shared a practice in 'The Rainbow Tablets: Journey back to wholeness' where you can loop your higher chakras together using the infinity symbol. This is also a practice you can explore to build the energy together, although it is more often used at the initial stages when you are cultivating the connection. Once this is established, the creator force of each of you will rise together as described above.

If you do not instantly reach this state of bliss as soon as you come into the heart, that is ok. There is often a process of building up to it. Allow the creator force within you to move into your Rainbow Diamond Cosmic Heart within. If you have not already activated your Rainbow Diamond Cosmic Heart, we have previously passed this activation through the Channel. We invite you to do this before taking part in this practice.

Using the breath and undulating movement of your body to keep sending waves of creator force into the heart, connect in with the bliss and wholeness. You may feel, see or sense the explosion of Rainbow Diamond Frequency emanating from your heart. If you are in practice with another, you will each be transmitting and receiving. This adds to the euphoria of feeling your oneness within.

159

You may wish to stay in your cosmic heart centre for some time. As the creator force energy flows and pulsates into your cosmic heart, you can access all that you desire. The heart is a portal. And your cosmic heart within is connected to the great cosmic heart. Through this connection you can receive great clarity, divine inspiration, guidance, visions, healing, expansion. The possibilities are endless. And once you become the state of orgasm, you literally experience yourself as the All-essence. You experience yourself as creation itself, as all that is, and as divine love – the Rainbow Frequency. This means you can create all that you desire. As we have said, only those who are pure of heart and pure of intention can reach this state. So, when you create from this frequency you are creating with love, from love and as love.

Once you have brought the creator force into your cosmic heart within, and are creating through the heart portal, you can let it flow as you wish. We will describe one pathway here. But, as we said, the highest levels of sacred sexuality cannot be taught. You must *live* into it. So, we are just sharing some pathways and practices to assist you in awakening this remembering for yourself.

If you wish to bring the creator force energy up into the throat chakra, you may feel a huge opening of expression. Perhaps sound, light language or song will flow forth. You may feel a surge of divine inspiration that is immediately clear, or comes into clarity afterwards, once you have integrated the frequencies. If you are with a partner, you may choose to share with each other great divine wisdom, or simply flow with the sounds of pleasure to communicate the All-essence.

If you wish to bring the creator force energy up to the third eye, you may unlock great visions and remembering. Again, this may be a place that you want to stay for a while, enjoying all that is shown to you. If you are with a partner, there will be times where it is a shared vision, or one will see what the other sees. This is not something that needs to be forced. It will happen where it is for the highest good. There may even be galactic or magical co-creations that take place, such as appearances from star family, magical beings and so on.

If you wish to bring the creator force energy up to the crown chakra, you may feel what could only be described as a truly cosmic experience. Perhaps you will feel, see or sense yourself as all of the multiverse. Maybe you will experience the swirling colours of a nebula or the formations of stars. Again, the possibilities are endless. As always, if you are with a partner, it is about taking each other on a journey – co-creating the experience. It is about experiencing yourself as the All-essence, having an experience of remembering and co-creation with another All-essence.

At any point along these energetic pathways, you can rise into 'orgasm'. But it is not about a peak and collapse. It is about becoming the orgasm. This sensation is actually your natural and most whole state. It is what it feels like to be your Rainbow Unified Self and to be in The Dimension outside of time and space, where everything is whole.

You use breath, movement and the heart to empower you to stay in this frequency and maintain this state. It may feel difficult at first as you try to move away from the physical way of experiencing sex. But it will get easier as you get used to moving the energy through your body.

You can choose to move through the whole pathway or focus on a particular chakra for the sacred sexuality experience. Always, it is best to draw the energy all the way up to the heart in order to engage your Rainbow Diamond Cosmic Heart and heart portal. But from there, you can loop down to the solar plexus, sacral or root if there is a particular experience on which you wish to focus. If you are working on manifesting something specific, you would bring that in as your initial intention. But remember what we have shared about holding a pure intention that is not limited by an idea of the form the outcome takes.

Sacred sexuality is not just for manifesting and co-creating. It can also be used for healing. And, of course, it can be for the sole purpose of experiencing the bliss and remembering of your true essence. It really is all about what you wish to create from the experience. There are no limits. The only 'rules' are that you come from a place of purity – purity of heart and purity of intention. You create with love and as love. As we have shared, you will not be able to access these levels of creation if you are not in purity. This does not mean you must be fully healed before you access sacred sexuality. It just means that you connect with the purity of your heart and intention. Again, to support you with this we have passed the Purity Codes triple activations through the Channel.

When you have cultivated the experience you wish, you can either finish the climactic state or add another layer. The other layer is to bring the creator force energy into an infinity symbol in your body. The cross-over point would be at the heart and it would expand out, as we shared previously. Allowing the creator force to come into an infinite circulation around your body is powerfully energising, healing and rejuvenating, not just for the physical cells and organs, but also for the spirit and life force.

There is another level still where you can connect into the master cosmic infinity of the Arraya consciousness. We will not go into detail here as that level of remembering and sacred co-creation requires a whole other manuscript. The activations, remembering and embodiment of these codes are very deep. But we reference it for those who have embodied the Lyran Golden Abundance Codes as shared by the Channel or will go on to do so in the future.

To bring it back to experiencing orgasm as a state of being rather than a moment of climax, you must move the creator force energy around the body. If it only stirs in the root and sacral chakras, you are likely to experience only a slightly elevated form of the sex currently practised on Earth. But if you move the energy through your chakras with the intention, presence, purity, breath and movement, you will unlock the greater cosmic connection within each chakra. And, when in practice with another, you will be the reflection of The All for each other, lifting each other to long-forgotten levels of magic, multidimensionality and mastery. When you are very embodied, the pathway we described will feel like less of a 'build' and more of a sense of switching on or coming into activation. By this we mean that it all happens more or less simultaneously.

Purity of heart

Although we cannot share the full details of the magic of weaving with your creator force, you can see that we have taken you right to the doorway and even shared some of the practices that lie on the other side of that threshold.

To recap, you must be pure of heart and intention to access this highest level of magic. This is because there is no 'dark side' to creating as the creator that you are. When you create from this space you are remembering yourself in wholeness. Your dark and light within have unified, and you are creating as the Rainbow Frequency – the essence of divine love.

You are literally creating with love, from love and as love. We are repeating this because it is an important distinction. This is beyond ego. Any old fears around whether or not you are doing the right thing, or are worthy, or anything else of that nature, do not apply here. To help you reach this state, we have shared embodiment and activation programs through the Channel. These will help you release what does not serve you and what is not in alignment with your true essence. And they will help you to reawaken and remember all that you truly are. It is a sweet and long-awaited 'coming home' to your wholeness so you can experience yourself as the divine All-essence that you are.

Possibilities of the orgasm state

On Earth, the purpose of the orgasm is often seen as pleasure or release. This is true from the base physical level. Yet, orgasm is not just a moment, but a frequency. The intense bliss and ecstasy are actually the remembering of the divine form – The All. This is why we say it is like a moment of touching 'God'.

You may be wondering about the purpose of 'becoming orgasm'. By this, we mean experiencing orgasm as a frequency and state of being. This is the state of your greatest magic. For it is the moment when you are outside of time and space and reconnected to, or re-embodied as, The All. It is your greatest and purest creator force. And when you harness this as a state of being, you hold your 'wholeness' while simultaneously in your current embodiment within the experiment of separation.

163

As we have shared, you can only reach this state when the heart portal is activated and open. When you are in the state of orgasm, you are, in a sense, a time traveller. You are simultaneously in your time and dimension and outside of it. You can journey to wherever you desire, without actually leaving. The closest description we can find in your language is the concept of bi-location. However, you do not need to physically bi-locate. Your physical body will remain where it is and you can simultaneously experience another time or dimensional plane through your energetic body and consciousness. That is not to say that you need to do this. It is just one of the possibilities available from the embodied orgasm creator force state.

You also become a very powerful creator when in this state. The true embodied state of orgasm comes with a sense of such heart opening that it feels like pure bliss. Some may have experienced this momentarily while working with the sacred plant teachers. It is the sense of being one with all. And when you are one with all, you can create as creation itself.

This is beyond what you have experienced as manifesting. Things can be instant or very quick to come about. And, to reach this embodied orgasm state, you have already released the illusions of limitations. You have already remembered that there is no lack or unworthiness and nothing blocking you from all that your heart and soul desire. You have remembered yourself as a sovereign being – the All-essence.

Because there is nothing blocking you, the infinite pure abundance consciousness of the multiverse – the Arraya – pulses with you. You become one. In a sense, you already are. For each and every being in creation gave a golden aspect of itself to create the Arraya pure abundance consciousness. So, as you create from your creator force 'orgasm' frequency, you are working as one with the infinite ever-flowing abundance of the multiverse.

As you can imagine, this can bring enormous shifts not just for yourself, but for Earth and other dimensional planes. If you start to understand the magnitude and power of this pure magic, you may wonder what would happen if it were misused. This is not possible. As we have shared, only those who are pure of heart, voice and vision can weave this pure magic. And you can only experience yourself as the creator force once you have come back to wholeness within. This means you are beyond the duality of light and dark. Everything you create is not just woven with love, but as divine love itself.

It may seem hard to conceive that one would be capable of weaving such unlimited magic and be trusted with it. But that is because you are accustomed to a world that is filled with duality, greed and corruption. This is the result of the old programs placed on humans and the ploys of the ego. For one to reach these levels of the pure magic, they must have transcended these lower realities and unplugged from the disempowering programs.

It is hard to explain all that is possible once one achieves the embodiment of the state of orgasm. Much of it is beyond your realms of comprehension. This is why we say the highest levels of sacred sexuality cannot be taught or reduced to words. It must be experienced.

But we can say that this is the experience of being The All on Earth. It is the experience of being able to effortlessly move through time and dimensions. It is the experience of weaving your magic and creating as the creator force. And it is the experience of being both an individual in your current incarnation, and simultaneously completely whole in the form of your Rainbow Unified Self.

This is just the beginning

We have shared much cosmic remembering in this manuscript. And it may feel like it is the 'answer' to all that you have been seeking. It might feel like the 'destination'. We understand that you have healed, recognised and unlocked a lot by reading this transmission. But we wish to invite you not to think of it as the destination, but as the doorway. Or you could see it as a springboard to the next level of your cosmic remembering.

We can share a great deal through The Rainbow Tablets manuscripts. But we cannot share everything. To come into the deeper levels of healing, wholeness and divine union (both within and with another) requires embodiment. That is why we say this manuscript is more like a doorway or springboard. Because, if you wish to embody what we have shared and experience it here on Earth, you must do the work.

The Channel will tell you that much has been asked of her along her journey. It is not just a case of sitting down and typing what we pass through her. Rather, she lives her life as sacred. She approaches every moment of every day with intention. Yes, she too has her moments of dropping out of highest alignment. But she knows how to bring herself back to connection and her Rainbow Frequency. Ceremony and the sacred are woven into the way that she sees, perceives and experiences the world. She continues to do the work on herself. And when we ask her to share offerings with you, such as the embodiment programs, retreats and the Rainbow Tablets Mystery School, she goes through the process of initiations and teachings in order to embody them first.

We say this because everything we are sharing with you is to empower you. It is to help you uncover and awaken the great cosmic wisdom and wholeness that you hold inside. If we were to position The Rainbow Tablets manuscripts as the answer to everything, we would be doing you a disservice. We are simply helping you to remember. What you seek, lies within.

So, commit to your journey and do the work. Invite in people and offerings that empower you and create the space for your own discovery. Let the journey of remembering be joyful. You are not failing if you are not in full alignment all the time. This is why we shared that the Channel has these same experiences. Being in human form on Earth is a big experience. You do not need to criticise yourself for not being 'perfect' or living up to an expectation you have created for yourself.

Did you notice the title of the first manuscript? It was not 'The Rainbow Tablets: Arrive instantly at wholeness.' We called it a journey because that is what it is. And it is beautiful. It is a process of rediscovery. How amazing to remember what has been lost for so long! How joyful to uncover more and more wonders and wisdom. This experience in separation has been 'big', to say the least. But this moment of remembering is more magical than any of us could have anticipated.

Before we finish up, let us share in the next section about one more mystical and expansive aspect of this powerful topic of divine union and sacred sexuality.

Section 9

THE HIGHER INITIATION OF PREGNANCY

My body relished the breeze of the fan as it oscillated from the mount above. It was so delicious to trade in the cold and dreary English winter for the Mexican heat. This had been my favourite café for the last two weeks. The outdoor undercover set up offered sun protection while still being part of the vibrant Caribbean life.

I waved as my friend arrived and stood to give her a hug. We sat with a flurry of hellos. It was funny. Beáta was a powerful and authentic Shamanic woman who had lived in Sydney for decades. I had heard of her many times, but our paths never crossed. Somehow, once I moved to Peru and she moved to Mexico, we had connected online.

This trip had been a lifeline. The grief of losing my dad after he had been well enough to go home for three months had been such a shock. His heart had given out from the stress of so many operations. Even though he made it through the heart valve replacement surgery, his lungs never recovered from being on life support for so long.

In those last months, we had shared a lot on the higher planes. He had been my guide to hidden cosmic wisdom and mysteries that I knew would be the start of my next big calling. And I had honoured his decision to move on. He had fought so hard to stay. By the end though, I felt peace within him. He was ready to be in service at the next level. But the world felt so different without him. And it had torn me apart.

I had reached a critical point. My love of life and passion for my work had evaporated. I knew the only thing that would help me pass through this initiation was sacred ceremony – something I couldn't access in England. Now, after four transformational Temazcals and one Grandfather Wachuma ceremony that Beáta had facilitated on the Solstice, I had been reborn.

"What do you recommend?" Beáta asked as she glanced at the menu. We placed our orders and fell into a beautiful flow of conversation.

"Do you know, I came to Mexico with three intentions. The first was to move through the grief. The second was to fall in love with life again. The third was to reclaim the passion for my work. I feel so blessed to have all of them met, and then some!"

I reached over to squeeze her hand. "Thank you so much for the amazing work you do. Your ceremony was the reason I came here. And for the first time in a year and a half, I feel like myself again – only more expansive and more whole."

Beáta's eyes sparkled as a huge smile lit up her face. She was such a pure soul. She had also been through many initiations along her journey.

"Darling, I don't know if we ever fully get over the grief," she said. "But we learn to walk forward with it. And we come to understand the bigger significance of death, and appreciate it rather than fear it."

The waitress brought our vegan smoothies and I took a refreshing sip.

"When I lost my son, it was actually a three-day labour. I remember being in complete shock. We both were. I was sitting in the hospital bed with my husband next to me, and the doctor said, 'You'd best be prepared to split up. Most couples do after something like this.'"

My jaw dropped open. "Are you serious?"

Beáta nodded emphatically. "This is how broken our societies are. There is no understanding of death or grief. If that happened in the Andes, the Shaman would come to offer a blessing and help the soul move on. The grandfathers and grandmothers would gather to lay flowers and coca leaves and sing. We're so cut off these days and the grief can feel crushing."

I realised how lucky I was. My work was all about restoring great cosmic remembering and wisdom to Earth. It was powerful and galactic. But Ausangate and Peru had known I would not be able to hold it without the right support. After all, the journey back to wholeness was the unification. Earth and stars needed to be brought together within. It was through ceremony and the Earth practices that I had found my grounding. It provided the container for me to anchor my ability to weave the pure magic and shape my reality.

If I had not known to go to the mountain, the pathway to England would have remained blocked. If I had not known to seek the help of the Ancestor Star Keepers at Uluru, I would have never had those last precious hugs and laughter with my dad. And if I had not known to come to the Temazcal and Wachuma, the grief would have destroyed me.

This is why I had been guided to develop offerings that shared this with others. I had been gifted something enormous from the ancestors, the sacred lands and the Andean wisdom keepers. But it was not for me alone. Not everyone had the courage or freedom to pack up their entire lives and move to the Andes for a few years. I knew I had been entrusted to bring this remembering to others. I had to share how to unify Earth and stars, and what it meant to truly live life as sacred. Only then could we embody the fullness of our multidimensionality. Although Beáta's expression of work was different, I knew that she too had been entrusted with bringing these tools and remembering to many.

"Was losing your son what put you on your path?" I asked.

"No. I was already working in this space then. But it took my commitment to a whole other level. I made him a promise. You cannot make a promise to your dead son and not follow through on it."

Beáta smiled and I could see her son's essence reflected in her eyes. "Losing him made me realise that love was the only way to heal such a traumatic experience. Love was the answer to everything. I wasn't healed when I stepped fully onto this path. But the work healed me."

As she spoke, my eyes welled. It was such a gift to be in the presence of such a true medicine woman. For so long I had known that all of us – men and women alike – carried unique medicine. It was just about whether or not we embraced it. My journey with my twin flame had been the greatest grief and betrayal I had experienced. Yet, when I had leaned into it and moved through it, I had arrived at a greater understanding of cosmic love than I ever could have imagined. Now, the grief over the transition of my favourite person on Earth had taken me to new levels of love and connection.

"Do you know who your son was?" I asked.

Beáta gave a knowing smile. "He was my twin flame."

I raised my eyebrows in awe. "Wow! It amazes me to see the depths of co-creation that can happen through the womb. Whether it's birth, termination, miscarriage or still born… all are divine forms of higher weaving. I never knew that until the spirit of my baby shared it with me."

Just then, our food arrived and we started to talk excitedly about the year ahead. Beáta was about to commence her Temazcal training. She channelled the most amazing songs I had ever come across. I couldn't wait to one day experience that within the dark and intense heat of the traditional sweat lodge. After that, she was moving country. My heart rejoiced that with borders re-opening, people from all over the world would once more be able to physically unite in sacred circle.

Our salad bowls were delicious and I scooped up the last of my guacamole. It was my turn to share. I told Beáta I was committing to releasing the second and third books. Plus, there was something new I had just agreed to. It felt bigger than anything I had channelled so far. Biting my lip, I wondered if I was willing to speak it into being. I knew the power that held. In an instant though, I knew I was ready.

"There is one huge thing that I just agreed to," I said with anticipation. "Ra-Horakhty came to me around the Solstice and told me it's time for me to bring through the Rainbow Tablets Mystery School."

Beáta's eyes lit up and I continued, clasping my hands together with excitement. "Two years ago, my team told me about it. It was while I was still living in Peru. I freaked out. It just felt too huge and I said, 'Who am I to do that?' But they told me it was a couple of years off. They were just giving me notice. They said that when it was time, I would be ready."

"Oh, wow, darling. This is wonderful!"

I cupped my cheeks in my hands and gave a little squeal. I knew I was ready. I could feel all that was waiting to flow through. There was a sense that after saying yes to this, my life was going to jump up to a whole new level. Beáta grabbed my hand and squeezed it.

"Algo más?" the waitress asked. Somehow hours had passed and we realised we were getting the nudge to finish up. It had been so uplifting to chat and be in sisterhood. With a huge hug goodbye, we headed off in opposite directions on the paved avenue.

Since it was my last full day in Mexico, I went to sit on the beach. At this time of day the heat was unbearable and I usually rested in my room. But I figured I should soak up as much sun as I could before heading back to grey London.

The sand felt amazing as I wiggled my toes into it. The waves were soft and rhythmic. I reflected on the incredible medicine this land had gifted me. Something the Temazcalero had said came to mind.

During one of the doors, he had offered copal to the stones to honour the ancestors.

"We honour those who came before us and gave their lives to keep this medicine alive. When the Spanish came, they tried to cut us off from our traditions. From our connection." The stones had sizzled, as though they too were remembering.

"The Temazcal was not permitted. So the wisdom had to be guarded. And it was practised in secret. Many lost their lives so that we could sit here today, receiving this sacred medicine of the grandfathers and the grandmothers. We honour the ancestors and thank them for this blessing."

At the water's edge before me, two dogs barked and splashed in the water. I took a quiet moment to offer my thanks. It wasn't just to the wisdom keepers of Mexico, but also of Peru and Australia. And to all whose medicine I had not yet experienced for myself.

Reflecting on what they had sacrificed, I realised how precious it was to be able to bring ancient and galactic wisdom to Earth. How could I have even considered giving up? Restoring the remembering and gifts of the Rainbow Tablets to Earth was my destiny. I had waited lifetimes for this moment. It wasn't just for all in the world now, and the generations to come. It was for the ancestors who had come before us. Their sacred medicine was supporting me in holding all that was asked of me. I owed it to them. And to the star brothers and sisters who were helping me from above. We had guarded this remembering throughout eons of cosmic wars. Now it was time to remember.

As I planted my hands deeply into the sand, I knew that nothing would keep me from birthing this work. That's what it was. Birthing. The cosmic codes that had entered my womb back in Peru one and a half years ago, had been nurtured within me. And now they were being born into the world, so they could help all who were ready to awaken.

I smiled and shook my head. How symbolic that it had been the Temazcal that got me through the wall of grief so I could once more live my purpose.

The Temazcal was referred to as the womb of Pachamama. The dome even looked like a pregnant belly. At the start of the ceremony, we would crawl in like a little baby. At the end of the last 'puerta', we would crawl out – reborn.

I placed my hand on my heart. Thanks to the Temazcal and Wachuma, I had certainly been reborn. Now the fire was ignited within me to finish the second book and let it be birthed to the Earth plane. The world was ready to remember the truth and magic of divine union and sacred sexuality. And I couldn't wait to share it with all!

* * *

"Bringing a soul into being from the higher realms is a powerful co-creation. It is another expression of yourself as the All-essence. This divine weaving is infinitely sacred. That is why we wish to share with you a different way to think about pregnancy, the deeper purposes of non-full-term pregnancies and the sacred way to approach parenthood, whether or not you are the biological parents."

The womb as a portal

It has long been known that a woman's womb is a centre of great magic. More than that, it is indeed a cosmic portal. You already know from the first Rainbow Tablets manuscript that, for man and woman alike, the heart is a portal. It can take you wherever you wish to go in the entire multiverse. It can traverse time and space. And it is the pathway to remembering that you hold all of the answers within.

Yet, when we speak of the womb portal, we mean this in a very literal sense. It is the way in which a new soul enters its incarnation on Earth. It is like sliding down a great chute from the higher realms into the physical realm on Earth. Each womb is a smaller version of the great Cosmic Womb.

We know that in the human sense, many women have trouble connecting with the potency of the great cosmic wisdom that can be accessed through their womb space. This may be due to sexual trauma, shame, cultural discrimination of women and so on.

We also know that many women grow up feeling embarrassed or ashamed of their moon cycle. It may be portrayed in their culture as dirty or disgusting. And it may be difficult for men to hear about this as they too have been brought up with these misconceptions.

This is all part of the implanted programs of disempowerment. The womb is a portal of ultimate co-creation between the realms. And we will expand on this further.

The cosmic purpose of different pregnancy experiences

From the human perspective, miscarriage, abortion and stillbirth are some of the most harrowing experiences one can choose. It is not our intention to downplay these experiences. One of the most beautiful gifts of being human is the depth of feeling. There are experiences that bring joy and euphoria that make the heart feel as though it will dematerialise. And there are experiences that bring grief and sorrow that make the heart feel as though it is cracking open.

There is beauty in all of it – the depth of feeling. As we shared in the first manuscript, the purpose of it all is experience. As a sovereign being, your soul will choose and call forth the experiences that will deliver you to the remembering.

As you have heard from the Channel, her own experience in this area was one of the hardest of her life. Yet, it was necessary. For she had committed to channelling this manuscript and walking her highest path. This is remembering that needs to be restored to Earth. But first, the Channel needed to embody it. For this manuscript is a transmission. It is encoded to awaken and activate deep connection and gifts within you. This manuscript is here in service, to help restore the purity of divine union and sacred sexuality to Earth.

As you know, this is the greatest power and way to weave the creator force Rainbow Frequency on this plane. Through the distortions and implanted programs, it has been stolen and suppressed from the human experience for thousands and thousands of years. The restoration of such powerful and pure remembering could not be returning through channelled words alone. It needed to be embodied. So, when the Channel agreed to bring through this transmission, she was, on the higher realms, agreeing to embody the remembering through certain experiences.

In this way, her pregnancy and experience with termination opened deep remembering that she could not have embodied any other way. It was a co-creation between realms – a deep loving service between the Channel and the being who, for a brief time, stepped into her womb portal.

We wish to now share the cosmic truth behind experiences of miscarriage, abortion and still birth. They are not random. They are not a punishment. They are not a sign of some wrongdoing or unworthiness. Rather, they are a cosmic co-creation between realms.

Remember that for a long time, the womb has been the main portal through which a soul can enter the Earth plane from the higher realms. Other possibilities include entering as a walk in or through a star gate. But the majority on Earth have entered through the womb portal. And there are many reasons that 'parents' and a 'child' – a sovereign soul on the higher realms – might co-create in ways that do not result in an extended incarnation.

Firstly, as you saw with the Channel's experience, the co-creation could be to support the highest path of one or both parents. This could just as easily be for the benefit of the father or adoptive parents as it could be for the benefit of the mother. In the Channel's instance, she was needed on the other side of the world. She had made a deep commitment to be in her highest service on Earth. At that time, her highest expression could no longer be served in Peru. We had to relocate her. It was in line with her soul's greatest desire and the higher weaving with her teams above.

Yet, during that period of border closures, there was no other way to secure an exemption for her to fly. She did not hold a passport that would have given her access to the only emergency flights operating at that time. Pregnancy or marriage to a person who had the right passport was the only way. The man who raised his hand to help and have his own highest expansion from the experience of divine union with the Channel, had not yet finalised his divorce. Marriage was not an option. So, an ascended master from the higher realms offered to enter the womb portal of the Channel, in order to open the flight pathways for her to come into highest service. This ascended master had completed its incarnations on Earth. But it was part of the Channel's soul group and trusted that the Channel would be able to tune in and make the right decision that honoured the highest co-creation.

As you can see, a physical relocation is quite a palpable outcome of the co-creation. Sometimes this is so. It may be the trigger to force a very tangible change in one or both parents' paths. Sometimes the parents will continue their highest journeys together. Other times they may need to go their separate ways.

It is not uncommon for relationships to crumble after the loss of a child, whether the child came into full incarnation on Earth or only within the womb portal. The dissolving of a union could be for the highest good. However, more often currently, this is a result of not being able to process the humanness of such an experience. As we are sharing, the higher co-creation possibilities through the womb are bigger than the one outcome of a child being born. Yet, this remembering has been forgotten. So, many parents experiencing a miscarriage, abortion or still born may become caught in the emotion and grief. However, when one understands the higher weaving, they can connect with the spirit of the 'child' and their higher selves to receive the deeper meaning and purpose of such an experience.

We reiterate that this is not about not feeling. Whether one understands the higher co-creation or not, there is much to feel in having these experiences. And we do not wish anyone to try to circumvent that. Often it is in the feeling and allowing of the fullness of the experience that the higher gifts and awareness are shared. But we do wish you to know that these experiences are far more cosmic and divine than you may imagine. They are a conscious weaving between the higher purposes of the 'parents' and the soul that steps into the womb portal for a period of time.

In this way, an experience of this nature could be a trigger for redirection or awakening through the emotional process. The reason or outcome may not be immediately evident. Yet, when one or both parents look back after some time, they will see how that co-created experience between realms led them to where they were meant to be.

Or it could be that the mother's womb or father's seed is holding trauma from this lifetime, another lifetime or ancestral origins. The soul may come in service to clear the womb space, so it is ready to receive the soul that will actually incarnate through this portal.

In these types of co-creation, the soul does not intend to incarnate. It is there in service. As you know, you have whole teams of soul and star family supporting your journey on Earth.

Another type of co-creation is when one or both parents have agreed on the higher levels to be in service to a soul in the upper realms. There can be many reasons why a soul would wish to be embodied in the womb space for only a short period of time. Perhaps they are healing some trauma from another lifetime and wish to be held in a loving womb as part of the healing. Maybe they are working up to incarnating on Earth but do not feel quite ready. Being able to dip their toe in the waters of this world enables them to move closer to full incarnation.

It could be that the soul has codes, gifts or remembering to share with the parents. If this can only be done through the womb space, then that is how the codes will be delivered – through a sacred coming together on the physical plane for the period of time that it takes. Once the mother has received these codes within her womb, she is able to work with them and unlock deeper remembering. The codes may even be for her partner, whatever their gender, and it is through subsequent sacred sexuality that the partner can access the new codes.

These are just some of the potential purposes and outcomes of such co-creation. The possibilities are endless.

In sharing this, we wish you to know that there is another way to experience these harrowing circumstances. We wish you to know that it is not a 'terrible' experience. Yes, it is an experience that brings enormous depth of emotion. But it is a higher co-creation. It is an invitation to connect with the soul of the 'child' and with oneself to be shown the higher purpose. It is an invitation for the 'parents' to move through the experience together, consciously and lovingly. This may bring them closer together or take them on different paths. But, when approached in this way, the choices will be from a place of deep connection and guidance rather than pain, blame or dependency.

Finally, although we are talking about the womb being the cosmic portal, we do not wish to take anything away from those incarnated in male form. As we have said all along, the penis is the key and the cervix is the gateway. This is divine weaving. The opening of the cosmic womb portal to bring through a soul requires the seed, at least at this point in time.

We also acknowledge the newer dynamics of opening this portal through surrogacy or insemination. If the parents are of the same sex, or there are medical reasons they cannot conceive naturally, this does not have to detract from the co-creation. Although, it can make it harder to 'conceive', which means 'unsuccessful' pregnancies may be more common.

When a parent is using these avenues for reasons of genetic engineering or vanity, there is no sacredness. Most likely, the soul who chooses that incarnation wishes to experience a more challenging path of remembering, or is in service to break patterns of disconnection within that bloodline or culture.

But, when the parents are approaching these other ways of bringing through a child from a place of love, ceremony, deep connection and divine co-creation, the weaving in these avenues can still hold the same divinity. We will now share more about approaching conception from sacred co-creation.

Calling through a child

Choosing a parent/child dynamic is a powerful co-creation. It is not something that just happens. It is a higher weaving. On Earth, it may be easy to think that it is a decision the parents make. It may seem that through a choice to forego contraception, the pregnancy just happens, and a child is born. Yet, in some cultures, a child's birthdate is not the date they are born. It is the moment the child is called in by the parents.

Bringing a soul into being from the higher realms is a powerful co-creation. It is another expression of yourself as the All-essence. This divine weaving is infinitely sacred. That is why we wish to share with you a different way to think about pregnancy.

We understand that in your time, it is necessary to take contraceptive measures if you do not wish to conceive a child. Yet, this is not the original design. This is only necessary because you have forgotten the divine weaving of the womb portal.

In the original design, being a 'parent' – a guide and guardian to hold space for a sovereign soul to come and have their own experience on Earth – was a conscious co-creation. When two in divine union felt the desire to step into the role of parents, they would start the co-creation. Until then, the portal was not open for a soul to step into and therefore there was no risk of unwanted pregnancy.

This conscious co-creation was sacred weaving. The parents would seed their intention and send the invitation for a soul to incarnate as their 'child'. This sacred co-creation was grounded on the Earth plane through a physical ceremony. This could be anything from offering sacred tobacco to the fire, to filling a crystal with the intention and placing it into the Earth. One of the most powerful ways was for both parents to offer their life force – the moon cycle blood and the seed – to the Earth.

They called the Great Mother and Great Father to hold the space and container for this prayer and sacred weaving. They asked their higher teams and loving ancestors to bear witness. And they buried their life force offerings with the intention of opening the gateway for a divinely aligned soul to come into co-creation as their child. Then they celebrated. They may have adorned the Earth with flowers, feathers or shells. And they may have danced and sung, celebrating the beautiful weaving that was being called into being.

Again, we wish to say that in your current day, this ceremony could be performed by two in same-sex divine union offering their life force. Where one or both partners cannot produce the life force offering, they can use something symbolic and of the earth in its place. For example, a woman might choose a red rose. She could hold it by her womb and yoni and, with her intention, let the energy of her life force flow into the rose. A man might take a seedling and, with the same process of intention, fill it with the love and power of his life force.

If their surrogate is open to the experience, they could also take part in the ceremony. Or, if the two are entering parenthood through adoption, they could offer thanks to the biological parents who have brought or will bring through their adopted child. The pathway of deeper sacred weaving is accessible to all. It is not determined by gender. It is for all who are opening to the higher cosmic creation of divine union and sacred sexuality.

From here, the parents would have made time to come into communion with the souls wishing to incarnate. Perhaps there was one that stepped forth and it was divinely felt by all. Other times, there were more than one willing to incarnate. So, the parents and potential 'children' would come into communion. They would share their intentions and frequencies. And when all parties felt the alignment, the co-creation was agreed. This could have been through one child coming through. Or perhaps there were souls who wished to journey together, so asked to come through as twins or more. Maybe there were souls who desired to be siblings and the parents committed to bringing them through in succession, so all could co-create for their highest timelines.

Then there was the process of 'conception'. If all was aligned, it may have been instant. However, if the mother or father had things to clear or heal, the soul of the child may have asked that this be done before they entered. Or, if an experience was required to trigger a particular clearing or awakening, the event of miscarriage, abortion or still birth may have been required first.

Again, the possibilities are limitless so we cannot illustrate all. But we hope you see the higher weaving at play. The original and divine approach to bringing through a child was not as it is on Earth now. It was a deep and sacred co-creation. And this remembering is available to you.

Over time, as you come into the new body templates and awaken the higher co-creation between realms, contraception will not be needed. For, the portal of the womb will only be opened through conscious co-creation. And, as we have shared in the section about Rainbow Earth, 'death' will simply be the conscious choice that one has experienced all they desire and is ready for a new experience on a different plane. So, as you see, the ways of entering and exiting the Earth plane are moving back to the highest forms of cosmic co-creation. These are the deeper levels of what it means to weave with the fullness of your creator force – the All-essence.

Parenthood as an initiation

From the human sense, becoming a parent is one of the deepest initiations one can experience. Suddenly there is another life, a tiny little being. The desire to shield and protect it can be overwhelming. It can bring up fears around failing the child.

It is this process that triggers deep ego death for parents. They will soon see where they may be holding unhealed trauma from their own childhood. They will be faced with any social, cultural or religious programming that they may be holding. They will have to shed their fears and doubts.

Perhaps most importantly, they will need to find the balance between their humanness and their cosmic forms. They will need to recognise the child as an enlightened and sovereign soul that has chosen to have an experience on Earth. Their role as a parent is to help guide and support the new soul as it develops and comes into the remembering of its highest purpose. This is different to old views of parenting. The old forms drive parents to be overbearing, choosing for the soul and pushing it to become the type of child and adult the parents consider to be 'right'.

As you may know from your own experience, this can greatly hinder a soul in walking their highest path. It can cause a war within between inner knowing and external expectation. For some, this takes years or even lifetimes to heal.

Yet, there is still the need to guide the 'child' through the experience of being human. As the cosmic soul 'forgets', it must then learn to experience itself and the world from this physical form. The soul will encounter ego, at least until the human DNA is restored and can hold the fullness of the higher self within embodied form. This process of experiencing ego can bring up anger, selfishness and other aspects of the shadow self. In this way, the parents will lovingly guide their children back to the heart. They will teach their children how to process emotions and make choices from the heart rather than from hurt. And they will empower their children with practices and tools to hold their sovereign space and cleanse their energy fields. This is why we say parenting requires balance between the humanness and the cosmic form.

The new Rainbow Children are choosing the most conscious parents that they can find. The veil of amnesia is thinning, so the children are coming through with more of their cosmic remembering. They can teach their parents. It is a co-creation. The parents can support the child's remembering and help them to ground in their gifts on the Earth plane. And the child can help the parents to remember their magic and multidimensionality.

The old phrases of 'that is just make believe' must be retired. For too long, children have been forced to forget their divinity and ignore the magical realms. Now parents are being called forth as guardians and wayshowers, being the vessels to bring these great masters to Earth and empower them to share their remembering of divine love, unity and magic. This is why we say that becoming a parent is one of the greatest initiations one can choose. Nothing can be left untouched within. This is a time of co-creation between souls as parents and children that is leading to the original purity of Earth. It is the Return to Unification, on Earth and across the entire multiverse. It cannot be approached in the old ways.

If you are choosing to receive a Rainbow Child, whether they come to you biologically or through another form, know that you are ready.

If you do not desire to have children in this lifetime or it does not align, that is ok. Not all need to have children. One may have already experienced that in other lifetimes. Or, they may be taking on a role where they are, in a way, a 'parent' to many. Not a parent in the old way, but a guardian and guide to help many remember their gifts and truth and feel empowered to step into their highest paths.

There is not only one pathway or 'right way'. Not everyone's highest path looks the same. You are creating your reality. And your highest expression is always supported.

Stepping over the threshold

What a journey we have taken together throughout this manuscript. It feels like a journey of eons. For, in re-awakening divine union and sacred sexuality, you are restoring the greatest magic and sacred weaving. You are reclaiming what has been hidden and suppressed for longer than you can conceive. Now it is yours once more – to remember and embody yourself as the master creator that you are.

After such a powerful journey together, we wish to bring you back to the purpose of this manuscript. You may recall that, in the first section, we set out to share with you the remembering and the key to unlock the highest levels of sacred sexuality for yourself.

As well as the big-picture cosmic remembering, we said we would gift you grounded tools and practices to bring about embodied change. This will prepare you to step into sacred sexuality.

We said we would expose the illusions – showing you the programs, distortions and ploys of control and disempowerment that are at play to keep you away from this remembering. This will empower you to liberate yourself.

We said we would take you into the deep and powerful remembering of divine union. This will show you how to embody divine union within and with another.

We promised to restore the remembering of the divine purpose and role of gender and sexuality. And we said we would unveil the greater mysteries around the womb, pregnancy and parenthood as an initiation and divine co-creation with the cosmic realms.

All of this was to reawaken within you the essence of purity and power that is beckoning you. The greatest and most pure magic. The act of living and creating as creation itself.

Now, we invite you to step beyond this threshold as the All-essence that you are, and into the higher magic, bliss and beauty that await you.

Author note

To access the activations and embodiment programs
the Rainbow Race refers to throughout this book, visit
www.sialanuestrella.com

Epilogue

The sky was grey outside and I nestled under my quilt on the couch. It was the first apartment I had furnished myself in over four years since I had left Australia. Candles, crystals and drums. Specially channelled rainbow paintings and light codes that lined the top of the fireplace. A super comfortable couch and chaise perfectly positioned for maximum sunlight. It was wonderful to have a space that fully held my frequency. I felt so at home.

My phone beeped and I smiled. That wasn't a regular beep. It was the PayPal beep. Someone had sent me money. I hopped up to grab my phone from the kitchen bench and found myself staring at the screen in disbelief. Was this for real?

Before I could login to check, there was a different beep. This time it was a message.

"I've just sent across the money. Can you please check that it arrived?"

My heart was pounding. Sure enough, I logged in and it was there. A transfer of 5,500 US dollars from my counterpart. It was money he had owed me for three years. In that whole time, I had only asked twice for him to pay it back. The first had been when I desperately needed to get to Australia to visit my dad. Then once more when my dad transitioned. Dad had asked me to do everything I could to help him recover. So I had spent thousands on healings for him, as well as doing healings myself. Plus, I had needed to take time off work to grieve.

187

Because I had actively released all anger and resentment towards my counterpart, I had been able to ask him from a place of love and non-attachment to outcome. But this was so unlike him. I was stunned. Perhaps clearing the energy between us had opened a pathway.

There was a message with the transfer. I laughed out loud when I read it. This was the amount he owed me. But he wanted to be clear that he was not paying me back. Instead, this was a 'gift'. I shook my head and smiled. That was more like the man I had known. Yet, the words that followed brought tears to my eyes.

"Thank you for your patience with me through it all. Your kindness and compassion have always been what stood out most to me. I still continue to learn from it. Thank you dearly for sharing that with me. May you receive all that you give many times over."

My heart flooded with unconditional love for him. I thought all the way back to the star gate in Peru when I had seen him sitting there like a lost soul. I had known that choosing to walk alongside him would be tough. But I always saw the beauty in him. It seemed that was a gift I had left with him. And I hoped one day he would see himself in the same light.

Over the following days we exchanged some voice notes. He shared that he had continued to treat women badly, but that it was torture to see the pain he caused. I had heard it all before. This time, though, it felt different. This was a man who had sent me a large sum of money he could have got away with never paying back. That marked a huge shift. And I was so grateful.

For the first time, I felt our chapter close. Everything between us was healed and whole. I couldn't help noticing the timing – just as I finished the book on divine union and sacred sexuality.

I had started writing the book a year and a half ago. But the journey itself started well before that. Just one month into the relationship with my counterpart, he told me I had stuck around longer than any woman in a long time. That didn't bode well. Somehow, we had made it to 10 months. My compassion and belief in him had been so strong. Too strong. In the end, I believe his higher self directed the cataclysmic behaviour that ended our journey. I was not going to 'abandon' my counterpart. And he wasn't ready to 'do the work'. That left only one option. He had to drop into such darkness that I could not possibly stay.

In those final days, I had faced a crossroads. Turn my back on my truth and step into the sex distortions in order to continue our relationship, or walk away. There was only one choice. Now I saw it as a gift. His higher self knew there was no way I could take the other path. And it set me free. That one gut-wrenching yet empowering decision had opened the door for the cosmic remembering of divine union and sacred sexuality to be restored to Earth.

Now that I had closed a huge chapter of my life, the future was full of possibilities. This journey had taught me to stay true to myself above all else. It had taught me boundaries. It had called me to embody divine union within, which was lovingly held by my two Lyran higher self aspects. And it had brought me into cosmic perspective and cosmic love that was beyond time and space.

Two days after receiving the payment from my counterpart, I sat at my desk to write. It had become clear to me that this moment was too divine to be omitted. The universe had delivered me the final story for the second book.

I touched my dad's ring and felt him with me. It was as though he were squeezing my shoulder like he had a thousand times before and saying, "I'm proud of you, Picci Pie."

I couldn't help but smile. The sun was rising. It was a new day – a new era. With all of this healed and lovingly behind me, I was actively creating the most magical stage of my life so far. The third book was already tapping me on the shoulder. The Rainbow Tablets Mystery School was halfway through level one and more powerful than I could have imagined. And there was so much more on the horizon.

My heart was full and life was joyful. I knew that, when divine timing aligned, I would be brought a man who could meet me. Not because I 'needed' another. But because I was so whole and in love with life, that I was ready to share that journey with another beautiful embodiment of The All. This journey never ceased to amaze me. I was in awe.

With a knowing smile, I opened my laptop and started to type.

Made in the USA
Las Vegas, NV
21 July 2022

51934840R00125